WRITING
ON BOTH SIDES
OF THE BRAIN

WRITING
ON BOTH SIDES
OF THE BRAIN

Breakthrough Techniques
for People Who Write

HENRIETTE ANNE KLAUSER

HARPER & ROW, PUBLISHERS, SAN FRANCISCO

Cambridge, Hagerstown, New York, Philadelphia, Washington
London, Mexico City, São Paulo, Singapore, Sydney

The author gratefully acknowledges permission to reprint from the following works: *The Dragons of Eden: Speculations on the Evolution of Human Intelligence*, by Carl Sagan. Copyright © 1977 by Carl Sagan. Reprinted by permission of Random House, Inc. *Drawing on the Right Side of the Brain*, by Betty Edwards. Copyright © 1979 by Betty Edwards. Reprinted by permission of Jeremy P. Tarcher, Inc. The Garfield cartoon on page 30 is reprinted with the permission of the United Feature Syndicate, Inc. *The Origin of Consciousness in the Breakdown of the Bicameral Mind*, by Julian Jaynes. Copyright © 1976 by Julian Jaynes. Reprinted by permission of Houghton Mifflin Co. *Plain English for Lawyers*, by Richard Wydick. Copyright © 1979 by Richard Wydick. Reprinted by permission of Carolina Academic Press. *The Reading Teacher's Book of Lists*, by Edward B. Fry, Jacqueline K. Polk, and Dona Fountoukidis. Copyright © 1984 by Prentice-Hall, Inc. Reprinted by permission of Prentice-Hall, Inc. The Shoe cartoons on pages 42 and 43 are reprinted with the permission of Jefferson Communications. *Spinning Inward*, by Maureen Murdock. Copyright © 1982 by Maureen Murdock. Reprinted by permission of Peace Press. The Fog Index instructions were adapted with permission from "How to Take the Fog Out of Writing," by Robert Gunning and Douglas Mueller, Copyright © 1985 by Gunning-Mueller Clear Writing Institute, Inc., Santa Barbara, CA 93110. *Apple II Reference Manual*. Copyright © 1979. Reprinted with the permission of Apple Computer, Inc.

Library of Congress Cataloging-in-Publication Data

Klauser, Henriette Anne.
  Writing on both sides of the brain.

  1. Authorship.   2. Authorship—Psychological aspects.
I. Title
PN147.K63   1986   808'.02'019   86-45383
ISBN 0-06-254490-X (pbk.)

87 88 89 90 RRD 10 9 8 7 6 5 4

To Jim, my own true love, who combines logic and sensitivity, reason and intuition, gentleness with strong masculinity: you are one of the most naturally whole-brained people I know.

And to Dorothy, whose friendship is a deep well of strength.

Contents

Preface

Are you a businessperson who is tired of wasting valuable time laboring over written work, a student with five term papers due in one week, all left until the last minute, a freelance writer with a secret desire to win a Pulitzer Prize? This book is for you. It will show you how to make procrastination work *for* you instead of *against* you, how to capitalize on times of incubation when your inspiration is at a peak.

Did you ever watch a colleague in your office dash off a memo or compose a major report with apparent ease, and wish to yourself, "If only I had such command over words! If only I could write more confidently!" This book is for you. It will change the nature of your relationship with writing forever.

Have you envied the novelist who has just published her third novel, has sold the movie rights to the highest bidder, and is eagerly working on novel number four? This book is for you. It will increase your writing productivity dramatically and teach you how to tell the story inside of you in your own unique voice.

The basis for this book is the belief that writing and editing are two separate brain functions and that the problems we have with expressing ourselves fluently in writing arise from doing both tasks simultaneously. The purpose of this book is to give you a new approach to writing, one that will first free up your creative side and help you to produce your best writing ever and then will hone your editing skills, when they are put in their proper place, to a keen edge. This approach will provide you with writing tools and techniques that will serve you well for the rest of your life.

Writing on Both Sides of the Brain grew out of the workshops I have given over the past several years, where people who felt anxious or unhappy about their writing applied these techniques and discovered dramatic differences in the way they write. This book offers the workshop in book form; it presents the same techniques I offer there and can provide the same long-lasting results for you.

Writing on Both Sides of the Brain will teach you how to fish, and will feed you for a lifetime.

WHAT THIS BOOK WILL DO FOR YOU

If you have a carping voice inside of you that criticizes your work and edits everything as you write it, *Writing on Both Sides of the Brain* will teach you to talk back, to turn your Inner Critic into your ally. You will know when to edit and when not to edit and how to go about it most effectively.

If you need to write as an integral part of your job, write for publication, or if you simply find yourself stymied by thank-you notes and ordinary correspondence, *Writing on Both Sides of the Brain* will help you get rid of the sinking sensation before a blank page. It will show you how to increase the speed of composition, introduce you to an innovative approach to outlining, and help you unlearn the writing habits that inhibit you.

My intent in writing this book is to change your life. I am not afraid to be so blunt, since I have seen the principles of writing detailed here work wonders in people's lives. Businesspeople, lawyers, freelance writers, doctors, teachers, students, administrators, lobbyists, elected officials and government employees—people from a diversity of professions—have taken my writing workshop and applied these techniques to their professional and personal writing with astonishing results. These concepts have radically changed the way they approach whatever writing they are doing. "Writing has ceased to be a problem for me," one of my former students said matter-of-factly when I met her again five years after she had taken my class. "I simply write whatever I need to write and move on to other things."

So that is my intent: to change, radically and permanently, the way you feel about writing and, consequently, to improve the power and persuasion of your finished product.

But the real power of this book lies inside of you. What is your intent in reading this book? In doing the exercises? What would you like to see happen, professionally and personally? What are your goals? Be specific. Write them down.

Take full responsibility for what occurs when you read this book, do the exercises, and incorporate the ideas into your daily writing. Make it your intent that this will be the most powerful, influential, exciting, mind-bending book that you have ever read. (I happen to think that this is a useful attitude toward any book you are reading, any course you are embarking on.) Decide that the change in you will not be just a slight one but a 180-degree turnaround. Make that your intention, own it as a goal, and then go for it, all the way.

I did not intend this book to be a library reference work or a coffee table showpiece. You have my permission to write in its pages, tack up over your computer or workspace the charts that appeal to you, dog-ear its edges, bend down its corners, use rubber bands and clips to mark off sections to return to. Follow Francis Bacon's injunction:

Read not to contradict and confute; nor to believe and take for granted; nor to find talk and discourse; but to weigh and consider. Some books are to be tasted, others, to be swallowed, and some few to be chewed and digested.

This book was designed to be devoured. I trust you have a voracious appetite.

HOW THIS BOOK CAME TO BE

A book that concerns itself with the process of writing owes a debt to its readers to say how it got written. I am, after all, doing what I am talking about doing, and in that way the process is different from lecturing. I am attempting to do for myself what I set out to help you do for yourself. I need to draw on all of my own devices in order to get these words on paper. Without practicing my own injunctions, I would have soon lost heart, and this book would not be.

Did you ever hear someone say, "I'd like to write a book, but I don't have the *time*"? In today's hurried age, people usually don't write books because they have the time to do it. I wrote this book while stopping at a red light, waiting in line at the post office, sitting by the edge of the pool during the children's swim lessons. I wrote it during intermissions at the opera, in the back of darkened movie theaters, during banquet speeches and luncheon lectures, in between family dental appointments and piano lessons and soccer practice. I have a reverence for paper and daily bless its Chinese inventor. I buy paper by the reams and still never have enough of it. I wrote this book on napkins, on the corners of placemats, on the backs of envelopes, on Post-it pads of all sizes and colors, in the several notebooks, big and small, that I carry with me. I wrote with anything handy (although I do have my favorite tools, among them two Mont Blancs and a 1922 Esterbrook, oblique nib). Later, I fed the written words into a computer, and sometimes I had the luxury of composing at the keyboard. I began each chapter with branching, a system of generating ideas and organizing material explained in chapter 5. I did all my branches in multicolor and sometimes used pictures as well as words to capture my thoughts.

I can write volumes in the midst of confusion, and I can easily write on the run. But I do need solitude in order to edit. It is hard for me to take the confusion out of my writing when I am surrounded by confusion. My environment needs to reflect my mind's work. When I was in graduate school, I would go to the campus library—especially my favorite room upstairs, where I was often solitary and could look out the Gothic windows and watch the tops of the trees sway in a storm—and spend as many as eight or ten hours in the same spot, pulling it all together. But I could do the preliminary work while I was out on a date. The same modus operandi applied here: I retreated for my editing.

THE TAO OF WRITING

While writing this book, I had a powerful sense of what the psychologist C. G. Jung called synchronicity: it was as though the universe was cooperating to make this book happen. Books that lay unopened on my shelves for years suddenly beckoned to me; I met the right people at the right time, thought of lost analogies; opportunities opened up; grace was everywhere.

Whatever happens, even crises, become grist for the writer's mill: a wonderful way to go through life. You might call it the tao of writing.

THANKS

It is traditional at this point in a book for the author to thank those who gave courage and support in moving the work forward. It is a fine and generous tradition, almost like the final curtain call at the opera, when the director and conductor step out onto the stage with the principal singers, when you have a sense of wonder at all the people who worked behind the scenes to make this piece of entertainment for you. If the true picture were realized, the electricians, the stagehands, the makeup artists, and the prop people would also appear and take a bow.

I am joyfully aware of all the people waiting in my wings who made this book happen. I would need at least the Metropolitan stage to accommodate all those who believed in me and my work and helped to make that belief a reality. First, I would fill the stage with a "cast of thousands": all of my students from ages five (Lisa, Jason, Paul, Amy, and Margaret) to eighty-five (Hazel, Eva, and Harold). They taught me while I was teaching them. Please give them a big hand.

Then I would ask particularly these people to come forward and take a bow:

Peter Scharf, the Macher—and the Matchmacher; without him the dream would still be just a dream.

Dorothy Harrison, my guardian angel, a rare human being who puts others ahead of herself, always. I felt the support and the power of her caring.

Tom Grady, patient, incisive editor, for his wise and wonderful way of knowing how to get to the heart of it. I wish I had had him for a comp teacher.

Jim, my husband, for his continual caring and love, and for showing me by his example that *wu wei* is the best way; and our children: James, for his strength of character, for setting his clock to get me up at 5:00 A.M., and for his delightful drawings; Peter, for worrying with me, for his encouragement and sense of humor, and for making "Never a day without a line" his personal credo; Emily, especially for her happy sign, bedecked with hearts and rainbows, "You have done more than is left!"; and Katherine, for her hugs and her smiles and her laughter.

Clarice Keegan, for going to Europe and taking my light pen and leaving me with her QX-10 and an empty house to write in, and for sharing her eloquent interviews.

Greg and Tracy Herrick, who make the best café mocha in town and have created in their shop, in the fine Johnsonian tradition, a haven from life's storm; Jeff West, at Creative Computers (need I say more?); Sr. Patrice Eilers, O.P., for her grace, in both senses of the word, for the peace she offered me at Rosary Heights, and especially for the fresh flowers she gave the struggling author.

The librarians at Edmonds Library, especially Millie Thompson and Lynnea Erickson, for their passion and patience, knack and knowledge to ferret out the truth.

George Kresovich, attorney-at-law, for seeing the light at the end of the tunnel and knowing it was not an oncoming train; for sharing his stinging, incisive interviews.

Richard Hobbs, for being a gift himself and for giving us all, vicariously, the gift of courage—courage always to write our best.

Mary Hobbs, my official *Christian Science Monitor* clipper, for not only clipping but mailing what she clips.

Elspeth Alexander, who sustained me with her wit and medieval brownies, and who, although herself a great grammarian, never took an ax to my idiolect.

Victory Searle, for her vulnerability, and for a life that lives her name.

Irene Artherholt, the first to look at me and say, "Teach me to feel confident about writing," who challenged me to ask the questions that led to the formulation of this work; with her support and good-natured laughter, she fanned the flame of my pilot light and kept the fire burning.

Mimi Bloom, who many a cold morning phoned me long-distance at 5:30 and said in the most lovely and encouraging voice, "Good morning, Henriette, it's time to write." And Dr. Susan Smith, who was also a charming part of Mimi's Wake-up Plan.

Dr. Joseph E. Grennen, medievalist and motivator par excellence ("and gladly wold he lerne and gladly teche"), even though he was the one who wrote on a college paper of mine—an analysis of *Sir Gawain and the Green Knight*—"a bit cavalier in spots, but on the whole a good analysis." The grade was an A, but to this day I am haunted by my tendency to be "cavalier." Sorry, Joe, I just can't help it.

Bill Harrison, for all the articles clipped and the philosophical discussions generated, for being a computer genius with a heart.

Nancy Ernst, my model and Muse. Kurt Vonnegut says we—all of us—write for an audience of one and hope the rest of the world will like it. Nancy, I wrote this book for you.

Finally, I would turn to you, the audience, and ask you to stand and be applauded by us. You are the ones who believed in yourselves enough to read this book and cared enough to make it happen for you. If there is any power at all in this book, it is yours to claim.

Thank you.

CHAPTER 1

From Panic to Power: Mastery over the Written Word

A mind that is stretched to a new idea never returns to its original dimension.
—OLIVER WENDELL HOLMES

It's time to write. The report is due (or overdue); the publisher is waiting for the next chapter; the boss needs that strategy report; the case is pending, awaiting your brilliant brief. Why is it that you would rather do something else, that you have a sudden urge to make a phone call or shuffle the papers on your desk? How did you suddenly realize that you need to do more research or that the typing paper is not quite right? Why is it that every word you write reads wrong, and why did you wait this long anyway?

Writing on Both Sides of the Brain has the answers to questions like these. If you are tired of putting off the writing that needs to be done, if you believe you have an idea locked up inside of you that you lack the confidence to share in writing, if you are holding yourself back from getting a promotion because you are not doing the writing that your chosen profession calls for, then welcome! If you are open to it, you will find here the key to fluency and the path to confidence.

I give writing workshops to educated, talented, articulate people, many of them professionals who are responsible for a great deal of writing. And they hate to write. These are the kinds of comments I hear in my classes:

I reread and scratch out everything as I go along. It takes forever, and I hate the way it sounds when it's done.

I was taught that the opening sentence is the most important. It has to catch your reader's attention, set the mood and style, anticipate the ending—all that in one sentence. Sometimes I spend forty-five minutes to an hour just getting that first sentence down, and even then I often don't like it. It's discouraging.

Why does it take so long for me to write? When I speak, I handle myself pretty well. I wish I could write as easily as I talk!

I need to have all my ideas lined up before I write. I want to be absolutely sure of everything I want to say before I start to say it. I don't want any surprises.

When I use a dictaphone, it makes me very tense. I don't want my secretary to hear anything that sounds dumb. I choose my words carefully. I guess it comes out stilted because of that.

It frustrates me to take so long to write. It always takes longer than it should, and that makes me angry with myself. After all these years, I should be able to dash it off faster and get the results I want.

My boss makes me so mad. Whenever I have a report due, he says, "Just write it. Big deal. Begin at the beginning, go on until you come to the end, then stop. Just write it. Stop wasting time, and do it." I just don't work that way. It's not that easy. There must be something wrong with me.

I agonize over every word. I would like to have writing be less painful.

I like to write, and I think I write pretty well. I wish only that it didn't take me so much time.

I love everything about my job, except the writing. I hate to write! You are a miracle worker if you can take away my dread of writing.

Wherever you are in writing, whether you like writing or hate writing, you can go higher. The work habit that underlies virtually all writing problems is the tendency to write and edit simultaneously. This book is about learning to separate the two functions: first to write, tapping into the right side of your brain for style, rhythm, and voice—for the sense that one human being is talking to another human being; then to edit, calling upon the talents of the left side of your brain, which appreciates logic, grammar and construction.

Writing anxiety is not new (you will see later in this chapter that I have personally documented it back to the first century B.C.), but it is finally being recognized as a problem that has a cure. *Writing on Both Sides of the Brain* goes beyond merely helping to surmount the immediate problem, however; it shows you how to change so that you will write as you have never written before and produce your best and most fluent work.

FROM STRESS TO SATISFACTION

This book will empower you to write well and it will show you how to shape your words so that they will have the impact you want on your audience. When you have power in producing words, that power transfers over to the effect your words have on your reader.

Before embarking on any journey, it is useful to notice and record your starting point. This opening exercise will establish your place of departure and help you set your travel goals. Where are you now? How many miles do you hope to cover?

EXERCISE 1: TAKING STOCK

In the space below, write down three words or phrases that come immediately to your mind when you think about writing.

Next, put down what you would like to change about your writing, what bugs you most about it, what you are putting up with now that you would rather not put up with.

Finally, write down what you would like to get out of reading this book and doing the exercises. Be specific. Write down personal and professional goals.

It will be interesting to go back over this list when you have finished this book.

INTRODUCING CALIBAN AND ARIEL

Part of your brain is out to get you. At least it seems that way. when you say, "I can do it!" a little voice counters, "Are you sure?" When you say, "Go for it!" you hear an undertone, "Don't be hasty now. Maybe you need to think this over." Often the voice is not just cautious but downright caustic. When you think, "I am going to whip that report out right now, and it is going to be the best I ever wrote," it knocks you off your feet: "Who are you kidding?"

This little voice speaks for the side of your brain that makes you bite your pencil, crumple your paper into a ball in frustration, cross out words as you write them, and beat on yourself for waiting this long to get started. I call this voice your Caliban side, named after the dark monster in Shakespeare's *The Tempest* who is part of each of us.

Then there is the unfettered side of you, where inspiration and rhythm reside. Credit this side of you for color and cadence and style, for fluency and confidence—and for those little gems of ideas that creep in often unannounced at the quiet moments. This side would be Ariel, Caliban's foil, the symbol of freedom and flight.

A third entity resides on Shakespeare's island: Prospero, the magician, who knows how to get the best from both Ariel and Caliban. He is outside of each, yet a combination of both, and at his best he recognizes that.

Caliban is not evil or bad; he just needs to be controlled. Perhaps he curses because he does not know any better. Ariel, too, can get out of hand without Prospero's firm guidance. Shakespeare seems to be saying that all of us are yin and yang, male and female, earth and sky, Caliban and Ariel, and we need those opposing sides working together within us in order to be whole. That is the kind of dual control and mutual cooperation that this book points to. When you learn how to make Ariel respond to your bidding, your written words will fly; when you learn to tame Caliban to help you on your terms, your final product will persuade with power.

THE CHALLENGE AND THE PROMISE

In chapters 3 and 7 I will present some possible answers to the curious question of why this Caliban part of you has so much power and why it is usually negative, or at least cautious. For now, I want to issue a challenge and couple it with a promise.

The challenge is to learn how to unlock the Ariel part of you at will and to train yourself to keep Caliban quiet until called upon to comment—first to write, fluently and well, and then to invite the critical faculty back, as your guest, to sit down with you in a nonjudgmental, helpful way, look over what you have written, and make suggestions for improvement, without name calling, without beating down.

This, then, is my promise: You can be friends with the side of your brain that is out to get you and you can be in charge of the inspirational part of you, too. You can learn to separate the writing flow from the editing or critiquing part of the writing process to produce the best finished product you have ever written. You can make yourself a fluent, confident, and effective writer for the rest of your life. Caliban and Ariel each have their place, as long as you are the one in control.

Let it be said from the start: this book would not have seen the light of day had I not in writing it employed the very techniques that I am inviting you to use. Following my own prescription, I was able to release the creative floodgates and let ideas flow—from the brain to the paper. The editing was a separate process. Caliban came back at my invitation and treated me with respect as I set out to review and revise, tighten and correct. And there was an excitement and an energy about both parts, the same excitement and energy that I will train you to generate about your writing. Your relationship with writing will never be the same again.

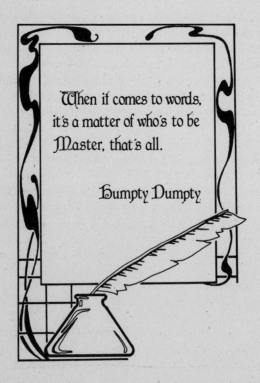

When it comes to words,
it's a matter of who's to be
Master, that's all.

Humpty Dumpty

WRITING ANXIETY GOES BACK CENTURIES

If writing, even occasionally, causes you grief and misery, you are in very respectable company. Publius Vergilius Maro, otherwise known as Virgil, started his epic poem, the *Aeneid*, in 29 B.C. and continued writing it until 19 B.C. That is an average of a line a day for eleven years, and even then it was not finished. You can imagine that he was not writing one perfect line each day and then packing up his stylus; no, chances are good that he was agonizing over every line and throwing out fifty-seven for every one that he kept. Some days he probably cranked out pages, while other days nothing came together. Sound familiar?

In case you doubt his anxiety, consider this: even after he wrote the *Aeneid*, he still was not satisfied. He left instructions at his death that the manuscript be burned.

So writing anxiety—a reluctance to put words on paper and a lack of confidence in those words once they have been written—has been with us for some time, and it strikes fear into the heart of even gifted authors.

I know an Associated Press journalist who switched from writing AP releases to composing his own book and found himself so blocked that, instead of writing, he turned to research. He studied in depth the phenomenon of writer's block, even unearthing an obscure piece about an experiment in Europe where students' hands were given electric shocks to make them keep writing. For three years he researched this malaise and discovered a wealth of information about the studies done and the learned conclusions reached. His bibliography was over thirty-five pages long.

But he wrote no book.

Why is it that writing often causes knots to form in the stomach? Why do we sit down with the pad or at the word processor with good intentions and then find ourselves immediately hating whatever words come up? Why did we wait until the last minute anyway? Putting writing in a historical framework and looking at our own personal history provide a partial answer. Just knowing the context gives some relief.

WRITING IS NEW—ONLY NINE SECONDS OLD

People put enormous pressure on themselves to perform; we want results, *right now*. There is no time alloted for growth after we reach a certain stage of development. Often people come to my classes thinking that they *ought to* be able to write faster and more definitively, that they *should* be able to express themselves effectively in writing—after all, they have had X number of years in high school composition classes, or X number of years of college, or X number of years of graduate school or law school. By now, they think, writing certainly *should* come easily. When they think of themselves in terms of writing, writing looms very large and they themselves feel very small. Anything that I can do to flip that equation around helps people to relax and, ultimately, to perform better.

If you have some of these tapes playing in your head, it may give you some relief to know that writing is new. We are just beginning to learn how to harness its tremendous and awesome power. For many people I work with, this idea alone is liberating. When you see where writing fits into the overall picture of evolution, it takes the pressure off you to perform perfectly and instantaneously.

Carl Sagan's *The Dragons of Eden* traces the fascinating evolution of the human brain. Particularly compelling is his "Cosmic Calendar," in the first chapter, in which Sagan compresses the fifteen-billion-year life of the universe into a single year of twelve segments. It would be easier to consider this analogy if our universe had only been in existence for twelve billion years, or if Pope Gregory had given us a fifteen-month calendar, but Sagan is not held back by such limitations. He divides his cosmic year into fifteen twenty-four-day segments; each segment corresponds to a billion years of earth history. Thus, the Big Bang is January 1; the origin of the solar system, September 9; the appearance of the first humans, December 31. The last day of his cosmic year is more detailed, says Sagan, because our history books are more detailed; when he arrives in his calendar at the evening of New Year's Eve, he is able to give a second-by-second recounting of the last seconds of the cosmic year.[1]

DECEMBER 31

Origin of *Proconsul* and *Ramapithecus*, probable ancestors of apes and men	~1:30 P.M.
First humans	~10:30 P.M.
Widespread use of stone tools	11:00 P.M.
Domestication of fire by Peking man	11:46 P.M.
Beginning of most recent glacial period	11:56 P.M.
Seafarers settle Australia	11:58 P.M.
Extensive cave painting in Europe	11:59 P.M.
Invention of agriculture	11:59:20 P.M.
Neolithic civilization; first cities	11:59:35 P.M.
First dynasties in Sumer, Ebla and Egypt; development of astronomy	11:59:50 P.M.
Invention of the alphabet; Akkadian Empire	11:59:51 P.M.
Hammurabic legal codes in Babylon; Middle Kingdom in Egypt	11:59:52 P.M.
Bronze metallurgy; Mycenaean culture; Trojan War; Olmec culture: invention of the compass	11:59:53 P.M.
Iron metallurgy; First Assyrian Empire; Kingdom of Israel; founding of Carthage by Phoenicia	11:59:54 P.M.
Asokan India; Ch'in Dynasty China; Periclean Athens; birth of Buddha	11:59:55 P.M.
Euclidean geometry; Archimedian physics; Ptolemaic astronomy; Roman Empire; birth of Christ	11:59:56 P.M.
Zero and decimals invented in Indian arithmetic; Rome falls; Moslem conquests	11:59:57 P.M.
Mayan civilization; Sung Dynasty China; Byzantine empire; Mongol invasion; Crusades	11:59:58 P.M.
Renaissance in Europe; voyages of discovery from Europe and from Ming Dynasty China; emergence of the experimental method in science	11:59:59 P.M.
Widespread development of science and technology; emergence of a global culture; acquisition of the means for self-destruction of the human species; first steps in spacecraft planetary exploration and the search for extraterrestrial intelligence	Now: The first second of New Year's Day P.M.

Put in terms of the big picture, it becomes clear: alphabetical writing did not emerge until the last minute of the last hour of the last day of the cosmic year—in fact, nine seconds ago. So think of your brain and nervous system as still adjusting to this new phenomenon, to the requirements placed on them by this new skill. After all, it's only nine seconds old.

On Sagan's scale each second of the cosmic year is equivalent to 475 years, so humans had fire for 396,000 years before the alphabet. At that rate, we should feel more comfortable with our backyard barbecue and our fireplaces than we need feel about writing.

Thinking in these terms can be very freeing. It gives you room to grow. Gloria, a workshop participant, spoke for many when she said, "I found this week I felt more comfortable about writing—as a new tool. Whenever I found myself getting tight, I just said, 'Remember, this is a new tool.' And it seemed to relax me."

So be like Gloria. Relax. Give yourself credit for even trying.

WRITING IS TAUGHT—THE BAD NEWS

The reason that we try, with disastrous results, to edit and write simultaneously is because of the way we were taught. I am doing it now, with all my training and background; even though I know better, it is a difficult habit to break. When you first began to write, you had someone standing over you ("for your own good"), correcting your form and grammar and spelling. After all, if your teacher did not tell you from the first day of school how to make that sentence complete, she would not be doing her job, and you just might get all the way to college without knowing an incomplete sentence if you fell over one. Keep in mind that at the time you were learning to write (compose), you were also just learning to write (form letters of the alphabet). Spelling, grammar, form, plus learning how to shape the letters themselves—that is a pretty tall order for a six-year-old who is also trying to collect the words tumbling out of his imagination, capture the ideas in her head, and put them on paper before they run away,.

So it began. As you will see in chapter 7, you no doubt internalized a great deal of this external pressure. Today, when you sit down to write, chances are that your teacher is still with you, standing over your left shoulder, correcting, critiquing, circling uppercase letters with her red pencil, and in other subtle and not so subtle ways discouraging you from writing, generally stemming the flow of words.

THE LANGUAGE LAB OF THE HOME

If we taught our children to speak in the way that we teach them to write everyone would stutter.

Mark Twain

What happened when you were a little kid and were first forming words? In studying that question, linguists, who for years tried to understand language by studying the speech patterns of children just learning to talk, discovered that they had left out an important preliminary plateau—what James Asher calls "the silent time." Asher, a professor at San Jose State University and the author of *Total Physical Response: Learning a Language Through Actions*, examined this first stage closely and looked at the mind mapping that happens inside before the baby articulates words. He noticed how even a young child who does not yet talk responds to complex commands in her native tongue. Our daughter Katherine's story offers an example. When Katherine was about eleven months old, she could follow compound directions. To test her sophistication of comprehension, we deliberately increased the complexity of the commands.

"Katherine, pick up that toy," we said, pointing. Then, without pointing, "Katherine, bring me your shoe."

"Katherine, sweetie, go down the hall to Peter's room, and bring me the red truck." (If you think that that is a simple command, imagine someone saying that to you in Arabic.)

Then, when she came back with the blue truck, we said, "Yes, that's a truck, all right. You are so smart. This is a blue truck. Can you find the *red* one?"

Always patient, gentle, and supportive—who would lose temper with a baby who did not understand perfectly?—we rejoiced in her proximate triumph, correcting gently any mistake or partial mistake.

Meantime, Katherine was not speaking in sentences. She was mapping syntax and vocabulary in her mind without producing anything more than sounds and isolated words, and that was okay. No parent of a year-old child is running to the pediatrician wailing, "Doctor, my baby can't talk."

FOR A BABY, WORDS ARE POWERFUL

Finally the day arrived when Katherine said her first word. It was not "book," as we had hoped. ("Book" was her older sister's first word, and we trust it augurs well for her scholastic future.) Holding up her baby cup, she uttered her first "real" word. Loud and clear, the word was "mulkie." For a nanosecond, all family activity froze. We were riveted to our chairs. All eyes turned toward her in amazement and delight. Suddenly, her mother, father, sister, brothers erupted in a frenzy of excitement.

"Katherine said, 'mulk,' I mean, 'milk'! Did you hear that? Give her some milk!!"

We gathered round her, rejoicing, called Grandma long-distance, and tried to get her to say it again.

Are you beginning to picture a similar scene in your own history and what it might have been like? Notice that we did not correct Katherine's pronunciation before we rewarded her with the beverage she was asking for and with lots of hugs and smiles and clapping. Chances are your parents and your sisters and brothers did the same for you. You did not mind making a few mistakes along the way ("Her go out"), and you were not worried about getting it perfectly, because the people around you seemed to be so pleased that you were even trying. They were willing to meet you halfway or more to figure out the meaning with you. Words had power: you said "milkie," you got milk; you said "blankie," someone brought you a blanket. If you had waited until you got the syntax and pronunciation perfect before you even attempted to speak out loud, you would be mute today.

I hope you cherish that time, because that was it. That was probably the very last time in your learning cycle that you were allowed the luxury of assimilating before producing, the last time that you were allowed to provide proximate results and get rewarded for it with great glee and enthusiasm. The silent time of thinking it through before producing is limited to babyhood and first speech.

Then you started school. In first grade, maybe you wanted to write a little story about a mouse on a motorcycle. But you did not know how to spell *motorcycle*, so you made the mouse ride a *bike*. At least you did not have to worry about getting your paper back with a red mark on the misspelled word. But somehow it was not quite the same story that you had in your heart.

We make choices in our adult life based on the same sort of reasoning. It is safer not to try anything. I know college graduates who had wanted to major in history, for example, and were fascinated by historical events, but had rejected it as a field of study because "there were too many papers to write." Or how about the adult who wants to pursue a law career but decides against it because of all the writing involved? Decisions like these, which limit our choices, go back to the first grade when your teacher was standing over your paper with the red pen.

So if you want to know how you learned to express yourself in written communication, think back not to your native speaking education but to the first term of high school German or French or Spanish or whatever other foreign language you took.

"Repeat after me," says the fluent teacher on day one. You attempt to repeat, the teacher corrects, you repeat again, your confidence wanes, your face reddens, the class laughs.

That is how we teach writing. And why, for many of us, as fluent as we might feel in talking, writing is like a foreign language.

MORE BAD NEWS

Since writing is taught, there are rules and regulations we pick up along the way that are meant to guide us but often wind up thwarting us instead. For example, I had an English professor in college who was fond of quoting *Alice in Wonderland* when students asked him how to go about writing this or that paper.

"Begin at the beginning, go on until you come to the end, and then stop," he said.

So that became my motto, my personal creed, and I suffered and agonized under the belief that step by logical step was the only right way to approach writing. It took me many years to realize that the process of writing does not always go that way; to try to pretend that it does is to impose an artificiality on your words that need not be there. Sometimes you need to begin in the middle and go back to the beginning and then write the end and then stop. Often you do not even know how the thing best begins until you have figured out the end.

The advent of personal computers and word-processing programs has helped immensely to give writers freedom in this regard. Even the simplest word processor program can "cut and paste," allowing you to rearrange sentences and whole paragraphs. We no longer feel compelled to think in terms of a finished product. Even if you do not own a personal computer, though, the lesson is clear: allow yourself to write in the order that things occur to you and then cut and paste, literally or electronically, later. (Rapidwriting, explained in the next chapter, shows you how to do that easily; appendix 2 deals with whole-brained writing with a word processor.)

WRITING IS TAUGHT—THE GOOD NEWS

Since writing does not come naturally, since it is, as I say, a learned experience, the good news is that we are always learning. It is not a fait accompli in the fifth grade, after which we spend the rest of our lives perfecting what we already know and learning the jargon of our trade. If, instead, we see learning how to write as a never-ending story, all kinds of possibilities open up. We have never arrived; there is always so much more to learn. Reading this book and doing the exercises is learning more about yourself and about writing.

Be like the man who was lost in Manhattan. He could not find Carnegie Hall. Finally, he spotted an elderly Hungarian carrying a huge cello case. Surely he would know where Carnegie Hall was. He approached him timidly.

"Excuse me, sir, could you tell me how to get to Carnegie Hall?"

The cello player put down his large case and, punching the air with his hands for emphasis, announced, "Practiz! Practiz! Practiz!"

NOT BAD FOR AN EIGHT-YEAR-OLD

Anne lives in Missoula, Montana. Her whole life has been one new learning experience after another. She greets each new adventure, whether it is becoming a plumber or studying the violin, with a positive attitude, an "I-can-do-it" spirit. Once I asked her what her secret is. She told me that whenever she finds herself doing something new, she thinks of herself as a little kid who is learning that task for the first time, rather than putting adult pressure on herself to perform. Instead of lambasting herself, for example, with "What's the matter with me? Here I am at my age, and I don't even know how to change the oil in my car," she pictures herself standing by her dad as a little kid learning it for the first time. And when she comes even close to doing it right, she exclaims, "Not bad for an eight-year-old!"

When you consider that writing is only nine cosmic seconds old, then it is not unfair to see yourself, in some aspects of your writing at least, as a little kid. Give yourself credit for all the good writing that you already do. In the light of these particulars, it is not so surprising that we have anxiety about our writing. The wonder is that we do it at all. So pat yourself on the back for all that you have written, and recognize that writing is a growing thing, a learning experience. It is going to keep getting better and better. The more you write, the better you get at it. Practiz! Practiz! Practiz! and you will get to Carnegie Hall. Meantime, it's not bad for an eight-year-old.

CHAPTER 2

The Hair of the Dog That Bit You

How do I know what I think, until I see what I say?
—W. H. AUDEN

"Writing is simple, Muffy," says Jeff MacNelly's Perfesser in the comic strip *Shoe*. "First, you have to make sure you have plenty of paper. . . sharp pencils. . . typewriter ribbon. Then put your belly up to your desk. . . roll a sheet of paper into the typewriter. . . and stare at it until beads of blood appear on your forehead."

Writing need not give you a bloody brow. The plain sheet of paper, the void screen, is what is causing the anxiety, so fill it with words. The best antidote to writer's block is—to write. The hair of the dog that is biting you provides the instant cure. Remember, the key to writing fluently is to separate writing from editing. *Rapidwriting*—letting the words spill out without stopping to critique or correct or rearrange—is one dependable way to keep the two functions apart.

When you edit and write at the same time, the result is often a disaster: a disaster for you as a writer and eventually for your reader. Purple patches come from the unrestricted pen. Go back and edit later. Later is when you invite the logical sequential strength side of you to come forward and apply all the techniques of good grammar and construction that have been drilled into you since the beginning of your school days.

Rapidwriting is sometimes called *nonstop writing* or *freewriting*. As all of its names suggest, it is a method of writing in a flowing way without stopping to reread, to evaluate. It is a way of holding Caliban at bay while giving Ariel complete freedom to tap into some of your most creative ideas.

If you have ever been in a brainstorming session with a group of people, you know the power and the creative energy that come from throwing ideas on the table without fear that someone will attack or laugh at them. Often the seed of a great and workable idea is inherent in an absurd one.

The essential ingredient to brainstorming—we caught on to this years ago—is that it must be nonjudgmental. Anyone in the group is allowed to toss in even improbable and unreasonable ideas without fear of being put down or ridiculed. The free-flowing and open-ended nature of the exchange creates a climate in which good ideas are generated; in fact, some ideas are born that I guarantee would never have come to light had the group not insisted on waiting until later to figure out their ultimate worth.

So rapidwriting is like a private conference—brainstorming for one. Get all the ideas out on the table, and tell the critical judgmental member of the board (your Caliban side) to suspend comment, to keep his mouth shut and his judgments to himself, for now at least.

Give yourself permission to write some "junque" as well as whatever else comes out. You will be surprised at the quality of the good parts.

MULCH FOR THE MIND

Giving yourself permission to write garbage is like having a compost pile in the backyard. It might smell a little and even look yucky, but it provides a fertile environment for some great stuff to grow.

A fellow in one of my classes had written only a few lines of poetry before taking my workshop. Six months later, he had written enough poetry to publish a book of poems. He sent me a copy of his collection; I was touched and amused when I read the dedication: "This book is dedicated to Henriette Anne Klauser, who first gave me permission to write garbage, none of which I trust is included here."

We put extraordinary pressure on ourselves and even on our great and famous to write perfectly all of the time. The truly greats of music and literature have disregarded our collective injunction, sometimes at the cost of much pain.

Once I went to a piano concert where a brilliant Russian pianist was playing an evening of Franz Liszt. He played the *Tarantella*, the *Don Juan Fantasy*, and *Liebestraum*. The music was celestial; it took the top off my head. When the house lights went up, I turned my attention to the program notes. I was still somewhat dazed from the power and the majesty of the music I had just heard. What I read there brought me sharply back to the mundane world.

"Liszt," the program said, "was a typical product of the Romantic Age. . . . He produced more than seven hundred works, including many that are either uneven in quality, superficially constructed, or downright dull."

Ha! Do you see the press for perfection we put even on our great composers? We do not allow even Liszt to have mulch for his mind. Can you imagine what it would have been like had Liszt sat down and said, "I am not going to write anything at all. I am not going to write one note until I think of something grand. Until I can compose *Lie-bestraum* without stopping, do the *Tarantella* from top to bottom, until I can let my pen fly across the page and never cross out or write something less than celestial, I will not write at all. No way will I ever put myself in the position of having some program notes on my music dismiss the bulk of my outpourings as being dull, shallow, and uneven."

Chances are he never would have written the soaring music that thrills the heart today, 150 years later.

So when you are writing garbage, think of Liszt. You may give yourself permission (or take mine if you need it) to write at least 600 documents that are either uneven in quality, superficially constructed, or downright dull. Once you get that out of the way, you are free to do the kind of writing that will make your heart sing and move your readers.

EXERCISE 2: RAPIDWRITING

Take a clean sheet of paper, and rather than waiting for red sweat, plunge right in and start to write. If you do not know what to say, write that. Write whatever comes to your mind, whether it is on the subject or off it. If you hear Caliban saying that what you are writing stinks, then write that down, but do not stop writing. If Caliban thinks you have chosen the wrong word, include that assessment also. Circle the word, and keep on writing. Incorporate all the negativism and critical judgment right along with the content. That is how I wrote this paragraph. Then I went back and crossed out all the static.

If your premature edit voice is particularly loud and interfering, you can take this freedom one step further by using what I call the "Invisible Ink Approach." Put a sheet of carbon between two pieces of paper, and write on the top paper with a dead ball-point pen. There will be nothing to correct, no way to reread what you wrote until you finish the page and lift the carbon.

Whether you write with this magic writing method or use conventional ink on paper, keep track as you write of what your mind is telling you about your writing. If, while you are writing, you are able to identify some kind of accompanying emotion, say so. Name it. If you feel anxious or bored or angry or energized, write that down as you go along. Locate your feeling in some part of your body. Do you feel a tightness in your hands, a constriction in your throat? Is there a flip-flop in your stomach, a set to your jaw, an itch in your nose? Do your eyes begin to smart and water? Write it down.

Include all your wandering ideas as well as those that are on target. Peter Elbow, in *Writing Without Teachers,* calls this approach *freewriting* and remarks that when you use this method to launch your work, you use up more paper but chew up fewer pencils.

The score is more than even. The words on the paper you use up will become more and more useful to you as more and more of the passages you write in this nonjudgmental fashion will be exactly what you wanted to say at the pace you wanted to say it. It is true that when you go back to edit (that is, when the Caliban Critic comes back at your invitation) you will find more in these spilled-out words than you thought was there as you were tumbling out the phrases. Sometimes it shocks me, when I am striking out the interspersed comments, to see how critical my early editing voice can be—and how often mistaken.

When that voice creeps up, we have been trained usually to stop— to bite the pencil, to ponder at length, to give up altogether. What I am asking you to do instead is to railroad right through, to keep on writing *for a minimum of ten minutes.* You will see in just a moment why that minimum is necessary. Mark where you *want* to stop, and keep on writing. When you look at that spot later and see the worth of what followed, you will begin to get the picture. You will begin to get the idea of how damaging and self-defeating it is to give in to the judgment of editing before its time.

Our motto is this: *We do no editing before its time.* (Make a plaque of it.)

EXCELSIOR!

Where was your marker? When you wrote nonstop for ten minutes, did you find at eight point five minutes you wanted to stop? Were you surprised to find a good idea just on the other side of that urge to quit?

Mountain climbers tell me that when they are making an ascent, whether they are novice or experienced climbers, they start out fresh and eager and then, right before the summit, they hit a wall, an almost perceptible place of wanting to quit. The novice will turn back, congratulating himself on getting even that far, unless he remembers the advice of the more experienced climber at base camp the night before. Watch out for the wall! she told him. Push on when you want to stop. The best is just around the corner. The summit is yet to come. Do not give up. Do not turn back. Excelsior! Ever upward!

Those of you who have had children or have ever assisted as labor coach at the birth of a child will recognize this as the time of transition. Transition is the time in the birth process when the mother decides that this is more than she bargained for and decides to let someone else have this baby. Then the father smiles broadly because he knows that this is the sign he has waited for, the clear sign that the baby has almost arrived.

So welcome the wall. Good stuff lies just beyond. Keep on writing past the exhaustion or the emptiness, past the urge to quit, and reach the summit. Think of me, down here at base camp, shouting "Excelsior!"—goading you onward when you feel as though it is enough, as

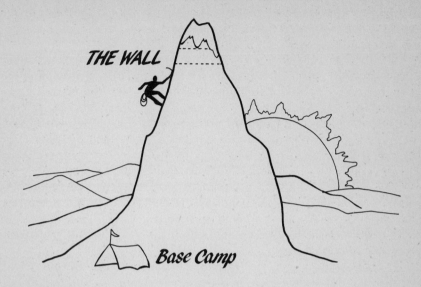

though you have nothing more to say. Excelsior! Ever upward! On to the summit!

A real-life mountain climber in one of my seminars told me that he plays a mental trick on himself when he hits the wall. He says to himself, "I know that you are tired, I know you want to stop, just keep climbing for ten more minutes. At the end of ten more minutes, if you still want to quit, then I will stop." Pushing himself that ten more minutes always gives him the "second wind" he needs to carry through to the top.

Adjust that trick to your writing wall, whether your reluctance is based on the flow of ideas ("That's it; I've run out of ideas") or actual time ("Well, it's almost midnight; I've worked on this long enough"). Set yourself a goal, "I will write until the bottom of this page," or "I will continue writing for five more minutes." Agree to quit if nothing happens. Go the extra mile, and you may find yourself covering a league before you know it.

PAGE 53 AND FOLLOWING

I call this picture of a mountain climber "The Beth Means Memorial Visual" in honor of a brilliant young woman who took my course several years ago. Beth had already written two books on DIGICALC, a computer program that helps you do calculation. Now, in the middle of her third book, she was stymied. She could not get beyond page 53. She called for help; we met at a French café. I drew a diagram of a mountain climber on a croissant-smudged napkin to show Beth what she was up against. It was as simple as that. Keep on writing, even though you want to stop. You can always go back and edit those pages later, but do not let the reluctance to move forward stop you now. Good stuff is just around the corner.

So Beth went back to work and resumed writing. For ten or fifteen pages, she told me later, her work was plodding and lifeless. She felt as though her feet were in molasses taking one slow, sticky step after another. She heard me saying "Excelsior!" and knew that the important thing was to get beyond the wall. Suddenly, a gust of wind filled her sails. Lo and behold! the pen started to glide along the page. She was like the Ancient Mariner heading home. The next 250 pages—to the end of the book—practically wrote themselves.

Then she went back to that section of molasses prose. To her astonishment, she found that it was not as terrible to read as she suspected when writing it. She doctored it up here and there, changed a few words, took out some extraneous whining—and now her book was ready for the publisher.

Beth called me and said, "Tell your students about the wall. And tell them that the difference between a writer and an author is page 53."

A *writer* comes to page 53 and thinks he or she was never meant to write a book anyway; there are a few good articles here. An *author* pushes on past the wall.

Excelsior! The best is yet to come. Think of Beth, and keep on writing.

AN EXAMPLE OF RAPIDWRITING

Here is an example of how writing past the wall produced an unexpected bonus. Marilyn is a college professor. She came to the workshop because she was having trouble writing a professional paper. Her rapidwriting revealed some things about herself she did not realize before she started writing. This is what she wrote:

This is how I see myself as a writer—in a tower somewhere, but I don't mean an ivory tower, but more an attic loft built into a house, filled with children and I like to think of the house as filled with laughter and fun of a big family and me as the mother and the writer—primarily a writer of children's books. That's a dream I have had ever since I can remember, but I also have this vision of myself as a freelance writer with a camera around my neck taking stunning pictures that are published all over the world—in my London Fog, I am called on assignment everywhere around the globe—sometimes I think that would be even more exciting than being a stuffy English don in the ivied halls of academe—English professors, professors in general are basically passive people, like mothers, they exist so others might be nurtured, so that others might learn from them and go on to greatness, while the professors stay in one place, and generations of students adore (or fear and hate) them. I am beginning to see myself as much more active than that—I want to be part of what's happening—the A's teach, and the B's work for the C's—so now I see myself in my wildest imaginings as a kind of Oriana—what is her name—Fallaci, interviewing the great and the famous, feared and respected—and I picture her of course with a camera, and epaulets of some sort, if not on her London Fog, then certainly on her blouse—like that great blouse I bought in Europe for the rail trip and every time I wear it, I feel adventurous and courageous—it's a secret we share, me and that blouse—I put it on and behind it, I am fearless (and "cool")—back to Fallaci—she is dressed in a blouse like that with long frosted hair pulled back with a long scarf—and for her, it's okay to be forty, in fact, *de rigueur*.

Sometimes the true power of a rapidwrite is not apparent until later. A therapist in one of my workshops wrote this on the first night and came up to me confused. "What does it mean?" she asked. "Where is it going?"

I seem to be very resistant to using the many positive influences and input I've had. All thru school I was told by teachers how bright and creative I was. My stepmother is, I'm told, totally intimidated by what she perceives as my great wit and intelligence. My father, a man I greatly admire, firmly believes I am capable of doing anything I set my mind to. I was a teacher of positive thinking. But still I manage to be uncertain and to intimidate myself with fears of failure and of looking foolish.

I seem to live my life as if there were a panel of judges watching and taking notes. I put on makeup when I intend to stay home alone. At the grocery store I consider the impression given by the items in my cart. I even scope out my garbage to see what an observer would think looking at that evidence. I don't suppose it's too surprising that the idea of writing an article, a screenplay, or even a (who would believe it possible?) novel, sends me straight to watching *I Love Lucy* reruns.

I told her to wait until the next day's session to see if it didn't pull together for her. You will see for yourself in chapter 7, where I quote from her interview with her Critic, that she already had the seeds of something here that only made sense in retrospect.

THE PROGRESS LOG

They say that it took Edison over a thousand tries before he perfected the filament in a light bulb so that the light bulb would stay on. One time, he was asked if that was discouraging—to try a thousand times and fail. "Never thought of it as failure," he answered. "It was only a thousand ways *not* to make an electric light bulb."

I want you to establish a notebook called the Progress Log to turn a light on in your mind and discover your personal writing pattern.

The name Progress Log (or PL) has been carefully chosen with

Edison's story in mind. A log records a journey, and progress implies a moving forward. Whatever you note, whatever you learn is part of a progress, part of your journey. Every entry is a step forward. So the Progress Log is a collection, a journal, a diary that records what is happening and what has happened with you and this thing called writing. It chronicles your past history as a writer, records your present struggles and triumphs, and anticipates the future of your writing life.

This is unlike the journal some of you may keep already, where you write your daily events or play around with new forms, record ideas or conversations, or watch the pattern of your dreams or the pattern of your diet. Journals of that kind are very useful, but what I am talking about here is a specific notebook where you chart your course and your progress *as a writer*. And you make an entry every day.

"Nulla dies sine linea," says Pliny—"Never a day without a line."[1] I have the motto, in Latin, as a deliberately florid plaque above my desk and writ in large letters across the front of my PL. Every day I write something, and that something often develops into the unexpected.

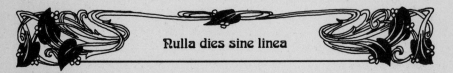

Nulla dies sine linea

Somehow an energy comes just from keeping such a record, even if you do not go back and pull the information all together and make connections. I can vouch for the effectiveness personally. I used a Progress Log for many years before deciding I had moved beyond that stage. Then one day I heard myself exhorting the participants in one of my workshops to use the PL and to write in it every day and thought, "How can I tell them to do it when I'm not doing it?"

So I went back to my PL, and my writing output increased dramatically. I cannot explain it, but just keeping track of what was happening with me and my writing generated an energy. Mayor Koch of New York was known to go up to his constituents on the street and say "How'my doin'?" I guess there was a feeling of well-being in knowing that he was even asking. The PL is like that. You feel good just to know that someone is asking, and that in itself will give you the power to write. Also, you will notice patterns emerge. You will see quite clearly what keeps you from writing your best and impedes your fluency, and what primes the pump and gets the words flowing. You will notice the times you write well and the audiences you write your best for. Once you are aware of your strengths and weaknesses, you are free to create your own moments of fluency.

EXERCISE 3: YOUR OWN PROGRESS LOG

Across the front of a brand-new notebook, write in large letters the words *Progress Log*. This notebook can be any size you wish, but it should be used exclusively for this purpose. Date your entries; it is often revealing to include the time as well. If you normally carry a small notebook, it is easy to jot down the ideas as they occur to you; either make that little notebook your PL or copy whatever you jotted down during the day into the big notebook at night.

What you are doing here is simply recording information. Let a pattern emerge gradually. Do not try to impose one or to analyze your entry psychologically. A useful pose is that of the dedicated but detached anthropologist noting and recording the tribal customs, cataloguing artifacts as you unearth them. No need to figure out what all this data means until you finish the dig; just write it down and later you can see what comes together.

What to write in this exercise? Date the entry, note the time, and then use rapidwriting to record what is happening to you so far. Where do you see yourself in your writing, and where would you like to be?

Now write down what is happening as you read this book, as you do the exercises. What was the rapidwriting exercise like for you? Did it make you feel anxious? Were you surprised by the quality of what you wrote when you went back and reread it?

Other things to include in your Progress Log might be stories that will come to you about how you learned to write—the good stories and the more painful ones about how your writing was received, how it was rewarded, or what happened when it did not please the person in authority. Here are some examples:

When I was in the fourth grade, I won the Little Hot Spot medal for the best essay on safeguarding the home against fire. I got the day off school and went to City Hall where the mayor pinned the medal on my chest while the Marine Band played.

Prof. W. did not like what I wrote. He tore up my paper in front of the whole class. I can still feel that rip go through me and hear the class titter.

Things are slowing down now. Maybe I need to take a break, or have I just hit the wall? Tell you what, self. Ten more minutes, and if at the end of ten minutes, you still want to stop, then you can, okay?

This is what the writer with the "panel of judges" wrote as her first PL entry:

With the rapidwriting, I found I was unexpectedly pleased with some of the thoughts and wording. A bit of it might even be useful in current or future writing. However I did feel a bit strained towards the end—my hand aching from the intensity—aware of others moving on to their third page—wondering if the time was up yet. In looking at it now though, I am rather pleased and I like the idea of doing this for ten minutes without stopping. I also noticed I am self-conscious about my uncertainty concerning correct punctuation and grammar. I feel it's important, but my formal background is very shaky; everyone was so busy acknowledging me as a creative whiz kid that I got away with murder. I think that's unfortunate. Perhaps it would be worth my while to actually study a grammar book or two.

When we come to the chapter on procrastination, you will see how dramatic a tool the PL can be in helping you break through writer's block. It's also a useful tool for generating ideas. Its unfettered nature seems to invite concepts that prove valuable in future writing, while its fluency encourages the sorting through of ideas valuable to any project. Several times I have gone back to reread a PL from years ago and found there a clue to my present writing.

It is better not to have any preconceived notions, however, of where the PL is leading or where it might take you. Go with the flow; I promise your effort will be amply rewarded.

Throughout the book, I will ask you to make additional entries in your PL. Look for this symbol: ▶ **Progress Log.**

These two simple techniques—rapidwriting and the Progress Log—combine to radically change the way you write. Take it from a pro who has been using both for over a decade: the more you use them, the better they get!

CHAPTER 3

Right Brain/Left Brain: What's It All About?

The mind is a mansion, but most of the time we are content to live in the lobby.

—DR. WILLIAM MICHAELS

Consider this fact: right and left shoes were thought up only a little over a hundred years ago.

And as it now stands, *95 percent* of what we know about how we think, that is, virtually all of current information about the chemical, physiological, and psychological functions of the brain, has emerged in the last 10 to 15 years.

Think of it. Human beings have existed, by most accounts, for two-and-a-half million years, and we are still in the infant stages of discovery in the remarkable field of brain research. Daily, new facts are uncovered, old ideas expanded, new directions indicated. What a great time to be alive! If we knew so little about our feet only a century ago, who knows what the next hundred years will tell us about our brains?

PUT ON YOUR THINKING CAP

In this chapter we will examine thinking—especially as it applies to writing—in the light of this decade's extraordinary discoveries about the two sides of the brain. I invite the reader to ponder with me the wonder of what is happening when thinking is taking place in our minds. Thinking: that magnificent, uniquely human gift that you and I share with Michelangelo, Leonardo da Vinci, Buckminster Fuller, Einstein. How can we learn to do even more of it?

This chapter may help provide some answers to that question. First, I will list the functions usually assigned to the right and left hemispheres of the brain, and then I will argue for using your whole brain—celebrating your particular proclivity and strength while exercising the parts of your brain you are not using to capacity. Next, I will show what happens in writing when we quiet down the articulate left and let the right shine. At the end of the chapter I present for your consideration a parable that sums up the unity of self and of society that we must aspire to in order to thrive in our modern world. Who knows how Harry and Harriet might, by example, point the way for others?

STYLES OF THINKING

You have seen charts like this before. Because of the early research that seemed to suggest more polarity than we now know to be the case, it has become convenient to refer to imagination, color, music, rhythm, daydreaming, and such as "right-brain" activities, and to logic, planning, language, mathematics, writing, and such as "left-brain." Actually, *locating* these processes is not as important as identifying different *styles of thinking*. I have made this chart deliberately playful and offer it only to help you get your bearings in the discussion that follows.

LEFT BRAIN	RIGHT BRAIN
sequential, step-by-step	simultaneous, multiple
verbal	visual
analytical	synthetical
rational	intuitive
time-centered	timeless
aggressive	yielding
objective	subjective
interested in details	wants overview
linguistic	musical
detects features	notices patterns

THE BREAKTHROUGH

The subject of right brain and left brain has taken the country by storm—hundreds if not thousands of articles, local and national, and several dozen books attest to its hold on our imaginations.[1] The implications of the research have given scientific weight to a way of thinking that in our Western society had been ignored or downplayed or even ridiculed—what is today called the "right-brained" way of thinking. The collective impact of the studies has made a profound and powerful contribution to our lives, opening up doors that had been shut for too long. Our schools, our homes, even our businesses will never be the same again.

The study of right and left brain puts twentieth-century thinkers in touch with our own diversity. It honors the different ways that people work things out, and it provides a springboard for using unconventional approaches to studying and problem solving.

Part of our brain was cut off, not honored, by Western civilization, and it was in danger of atrophy. Recognizing different thinking styles has put the whole person back in the driver's seat.

CALIBAN AND ARIEL ARE LEFT BRAIN AND RIGHT

So, to speak in terms of right and left brain (or hemispheres) is another way of expressing the phenomena that I have been calling Ariel and Caliban, of paying attention to the fact that one part of your brain works best for ideas and one part helps with editing and structure. This division of labor is not strict, but it is a useful way of talking about and therefore coming to grips with the mental process that goes on when we move from idea to final written product, communicating that idea to another human being.

The truth is, most of us are not using our brains to capacity, not because the capability is not there or because we are dumb but because we have not been taught how.

The underlying message of all the studies is loud and clear: what we are striving for is to be "whole-brained," to encourage a mutual respect, as a society and as an individual brain, for what each side of the brain can do, to have a willingness to work together in cooperation and confidence. The goal of "whole-brained thinking" is a call for both sides of our brain to work together for the common good.

Don't be content to live in the anteroom! Come, explore the mansion of your mind.

RIGHT BRAIN + LEFT BRAIN = WHOLE BRAIN

The two halves of the brain are connected, at the cerebral (upper) part, by the *corpus callosum*, a mass of fibers bundled like a telephone cable. The power and the range of activity of this commissural bond are far more astonishing than any mere telephone cable, however. Carl Sagan, in *The Dragons of Eden*, refers to the corpus callosum as a complex cabling system, "a bundle of two hundred million neural fibers processing something like several billion bits per second between the two cerebral hemispheres."[2]

Ideally, what we want (in fact, what EEG's show takes place in any highly creative thinking) are ideas to crackle across those wires—an almost tangible arc of activity, back and forth, back and forth, as idea and its implementation enhance and encourage each other, generating energy in mutual support and admiration. This "whole-brained" activity is the full genius of Michelangelo's Sistine Chapel (magnificent art combined with extraordinary logic and planning) or Einstein's Theory of Relativity (the backbone of physics, first conceived while daydreaming about a sunbeam in his eye). Honoring the left hemisphere inordinately completely overlooks the fact that these and other great scientific and artistic achievements of our culture have been produced through an interaction of *both* hemispheres in mutual cooperation.

Princeton scholar Julian Jaynes says that Einstein got so many good ideas while shaving that he needed to move the razor slowly "lest he cut himself with surprise." Jaynes also quotes a British physicist as saying that the greatest scientific and mathematical discoveries are commonly made in the three B's: the *Bed*, the *Bath*, and the *Bus*.

Einstein, da Vinci, Poincaré, Bernini, Buckminster Fuller, Beethoven—these are giants of their fields, and each one of them left notebooks or stories behind that clearly show it was intuition as well as logic, rhythm combined with structure, daydreaming coupled with careful planning, imagination teamed with evaluation that constituted his particular genius.

In common everyday experiences we ordinary mortals also activate this dual energy. For example, when you are composing poetry, the right side of the brain generates the flow of words tumbling forth and keeps the beat; the left side helps out with the rhyme (that is, any rhyme that is "thought out" and not spontaneous). Generally speaking, it is the right hemisphere that remembers a person's face, while the left remembers the name. The corpus callosum assists in this cooperative exchange, and the two halves of the brain work together as partners, as in this dialogue:

Right: Oh! that face! I know I've seen it before. It's so familiar.

Left: That moustache is unmistakable. What's his name? Where do I know him from? Not from church, or from the golf course . . . .

Right: Wait a minute. Let me picture him in his natural habitat. . . . Where have I seen him? Hmmm. I see him standing behind a counter in a busy store.

Left: The grocery store? The post office?

Right: Oh, wait a minute. Somehow I associate the colors green and gold with him, and I remember something to do with tools. Now I know. He wears a gold and green smock. That's the uniform at Smiley's Hardware Store. I can just see him standing there behind the counter at the hardware store. I can even see his name tag: "Bob Jones."

(Click into the "here and now.")

Left: Hi, Bob! How's the nuts and bolts business?

As for our writing, it is at its best when we know how to tap into the respective strengths of both halves of our brain at the appropriate times, when we remember to acknowledge the contribution that *each* side makes and have them walk alongside each other as companions, not as enemies in opposition. Unfortunately, there is a block against this wholeness, and that block usually comes from the left hemisphere lording it over the contribution of the right. As I've noted, in Western society in particular, right-brained kinds of thinking—intuition, speculation, and others of that sort—have generally been ridiculed or downplayed. So before we can celebrate this glorious freeing unity, most of us need to deal with a part of our brain (wherever it is located) that does not allow the other part equal play, that does not support, encourage, invite, and credit the contribution of its opposite number.

THE "KNOW-IT-ALL" AND THE SILENT PARTNER

In *Drawing on the Right Side of the Brain* Betty Edwards calls the left hemisphere the "know-it-all side"; Thomas Blakeslee in *Right Brain* refers to the right hemisphere as the "silent partner." These labels are appropriate because the left expresses itself logically and in words; this articulation is often carping. The right expresses itself randomly—in pictures, patterns, rhythms—and cannot articulate in words.

When it comes to writing, especially, the left brain thinks it knows everything. The fact is inescapable: language, verbal and written, is a left hemisphere "specialty." More than ever, Mr. Know-it-all is going to kick sand in the face of any suggestions that the right side might haltingly make. It is true that the logical left deserves the credit for grammar, punctuation, format—all essential to writing anything readable. But the right hemisphere has *style*. It has rhythm. It has the flow and the energy of excitement when you're on a roll. It provides images and analogies, color and music—in short, everything that lifts your written piece, whether it is a short story, a legal brief, or an office memorandum, from the mundane and predictable to the inspired and inspiring, the unforgettable. That does not mean we don't need the left—it simply asks the left to credit the right in turn for its contribution to writing. Any truly effective piece has exercised *both* sides of the brain. The music of the right hemisphere of your brain, combined with the rhetoric skills of the left, assures that your words have impact—that they are affective as well as effective. But first you have to let that music out.

SHINING STARS

The stars are out all the time. Why is it that we can only see them at night? Because there is too much interference from the sun. The right hemisphere is like that. It constantly sends us messages, but there is too much static going on for us to notice.[3]

When we quiet down Caliban, we bring Ariel out of hiding. But the entrance is tentative and timid. Say Boo! and the stars disappear. In this interaction between Jon and his well-known cat, Garfield, cartoonist Jim Davis underlines a truth that is deeper than the simple injunction "Don't discourage." He is also giving a dramatic analogue of how the left side of the brain interferes with flow and confidence.

In *The Inner Game of Tennis* Tim Gallwey demonstrates this same principle, "if you don't mind a little underhanded gamesmanship." The quickest way, he asserts, to ruin a player's game is to draw attention to his fine performance in the middle of the set. As you are changing nets, you point out how well he is doing.

"George, I don't know what it is about your game today! You're terrific! Tell me the truth. Are you holding the racket differently? Is it your wrist action? What's your secret, George?"

George is beaming. Little does he know you just killed whatever it was that was giving him flow. Now the left hemisphere takes charge. "Okay, George. Don't blow it now. Keep your wrist limp. Hold the racket tight, but not too tight. That's it now. Keep it up."

You have ruined his game, in the same way that Jon made his cat fall flat on his face. Gallwey does not use the terms left and right brain; rather, he talks about Self 1 and Self 2. Self 2 goes with the flow; form and figure are one. Self 1 reminds you how to hold the racket and provides a steady stream of comment on the action. Listening to the chatter and reprimands of Self 1 can actually ruin your form and certainly undermine your confidence.

The same thing happens in writing. As soon as we let in the critical, evaluating, editorial voice simultaneously with the performance, we fall flat. When you hear that voice, you stop writing. You stop and ponder, you stop and question, you stop and criticize, or you simply give up and stop altogether. You interrupt the flow. Rather than giving life and energy to your writing, such interference makes it plodding and predictable or, worse, stalemated.

On the other hand, wonderful things happen when you quiet down the noisy left and let the stars shine. Here are some examples.

Stand on Your Head and Get a Different View of Things

In her landmark books on drawing, Betty Edwards gives an unconventional answer to those who say, "I can't draw." She shows that all of us can draw, if we are willing to let go of our traditional approach.

One of her better-known exercises is the instruction to draw something upside down. Her students first copy a picture that is right side up. In her book the study used is Picasso's *Portrait of Igor Stravinsky*. The results from the unpracticed hand are usually pretty primitive. then she tells them to turn the picture upside down and follow the curves, instead of trying to draw an elbow or a chair leg. When the students turn their finished product right side up and compare it with the first sketch, they find that the upside down piece is invariably dramatically superior to the first attempt.

Author/artist Edwards muses:

This puzzle puts the logical left brain into a logical box: how to account for this sudden ability to draw well, when it (the know-it-all left hemisphere) has been eased out of the task. The left brain, which admires a job well done, must now consider the possibility that the disdained right brain is *good at drawing*.

More seriously speaking, a plausible explanation of the illogical result is that the left brain refused the task of processing the upside-down image. Presumably, the left hemisphere, confused and blocked by the unfamiliar image and unable to name or symbolize as usual, turned off, and the job passed over to the right hemisphere.[4]

What happens in art also happens in writing. The unconventional approach produces dramatically superior results, leading to confidence and fluency, as the left brain is forced to admit, however grudgingly at first, that the right brain did it well.

A reporter from the *Seattle Times* was in a workshop of mine right after the eruption of Mount St. Helens. She was one of the people sent to cover this momentous story. Before she left, they had a meeting in the City Room. This is not a print story, they were told. This is a story for TV cameras and magazine photographers. Do the best you can. So she went, and hovered over the crater in a helicopter, and then drove down what was left of the mountainside in a bumpy, open jeep. The devastation was everywhere. She tried to describe it.

"It is like the moon. . . ."—no, that would not do; she had never been to the moon, although she had seen the pictures.

"It is like hell. . . ."—but who had been there and back to tell that tale?

Finally, her left brain refused to process the image, and she wrote flowingly about her inability to describe the scene, the store of stock images that no longer served.

When the piece came out on the front page of the paper the next morning, the response was immediate. One reader summed it up by saying, "I have seen all the pictures in the magazines and papers; I have been mesmerized by the TV coverage. But I never understood the depth of the destruction, the bleakness and the unreality of it, until I read your piece in this morning's *Times*."

Maybe it was a print story after all.

Telephone Poles in Wisconsin

There have been times in my life, too, when I wanted to record in words a scene that struck me and my brain said no, you cannot do it justice: only a camera or a paintbrush could capture this. Once was on a cross-country train ride, passing through Glacier Park, Montana, at 4 A.M. I ignored the negative injunction and just plowed through:

This morning at about 4 A.M. we passed through Glacier Park, Montana. Jim and I were both awake, so we went up to the dome car to drink in the unreal sight. It was not pitch-dark, but early-morning dark, and we could make out miles and miles of mountains and evergreens dusted in snow. The snow was fresh and newly fallen, unsullied, and exquisite—so still, so lovely, with an ethereal quality about it at that early hour. The conductor was coming through the cars, swinging a train lantern; all else was sleeping and still. The train sped on through the winter wonderland, all the more extraordinary for having just left behind the budding spring of Virginia, New York, and New Jersey.

Those words, in spite of my belief that I could not do the scene justice, today evoke it more powerfully for me than any static celluloid image might.

Jerry-Mac Johnston, a playwright in my course, hearing of my experience, remembered a train ride from years ago when he had listened to the Caliban left brain and had not even attempted to describe an image that still haunted him. Looking out the window as the train passed through Wisconsin, he saw row after row of large telephone poles lying alongside the tracks. Although it did not make much sense, the sight of those huge poles lying helpless in the snow moved him. He decided to write a poem about it. That is when he started getting enormous static.

—It's just a bunch of telephone poles, so what? Where is the poetry in that?

—Maybe you could take a picture. Some interesting lines there. But it cannot be described in words, and even if it could, you wouldn't be the one who could do it.

Jerry-Mac listened to his carping critical voice and did not write the poem inside of him.

After he had told me this story, I pointed out that it was not too late to write that poem. You can go back to that time, I told him, and make it happen for you again; you can be at the scene once more, and this time, you can ignore the voice that tells you not to write.

I had him relax and imagine himself back on that train, capturing every detail possible in his mind's eye—the sound of the wheels clacking underneath, the rhythm and sense of movement, the smell and the sight and the sound of it. Now tell the inner voice to bug off, I said, and write in spite of it.

This is what he wrote:

> Derelict now in their duties
> The metal towers lay face down
>   in the winter's shrubbery
>   along the right of way
> It was as if a giant scythe
> Was clearing the way
>   for final doom
> Or at least
>   the end of electricity
>   in Wisconsin

Jon is wrong. Using both sides of the brain, cats *can* walk on their hind feet.

Whether you choose to call it Caliban and Ariel or think it sounds better to use the labels left brain and right brain, the important thing is to realize that what you have is there all along. To be whole-brained, you need only quiet down the noisy static side of you and listen to your own imagination. Then invite the evaluator back on your own terms.

Now here's the parable.

HARRY AND HARRIET: A MODERN PARABLE

Harry wasn't a bad sort; in fact, he was quite bright. He just needed to learn some manners. Harriet was bright, too, in her way; she was just too timid for her own—and Harry's—good.

At first, Harry and Harriet were a perfect match. They worked well together. Harriet had a great feel for colors in decorating, for example; Harry helped with measurements and execution. Harry liked numbers and was good at math. He balanced the checkbook and was punctual.

He knew how to plan things carefully, step by step, while Harriet was talented at seeing the big picture. Harriet was often late for appointments and sometimes got so involved in a project that she completely lost track of time, but she liked music and had a natural rhythm that was quite attractive. Harry liked to listen to her singing. He was attracted to her because she was so spontaneous and so playful.

"She's so carefree and imaginative," he said. "I love her *joie de vivre*." She sighed and looked up to him.

"He's so steady, so sure. I love his stability."

Then something soured.

"He's so rigid and unbending," thought Harriet.

"She's so flighty and careless," thought Harry.

Soon Harry started shouting a lot, and Harriet withdrew.

Quite frankly, Harry thought of himself as the brains behind the operation without realizing that was only half true. He *was* the more vocal member of the team and was certainly more rational, but still, Harriet was the one with the most creativity, and she had an intuitive sense about things that was often very useful.

Harry never took a vacation; there was too much work to do and nobody else to do it (so he thought). He felt overworked, while Harriet felt underappreciated. She knew her talents were not being used to their fullest potential. Sometimes it was very frustrating for Harriet; here was Harry ranting and raving, and if only he'd quiet down and pay attention, she had a brilliant solution.

Soon Harriet stopped suggesting ideas; Harry never listened anyway, and when he did listen he laughed or dismissed her ideas as foolish or told her, yeah, yeah, that's a good idea, Harriet, but then he didn't write it down, and nothing ever came of it. Harry was becoming apoplectic: life was a series of mazes with nothing but dead ends, and it seemed as though there was no one to help him, to bring any fresh life into his routine. Was he the only one of the team who cared if things were done correctly and on time?

Something had to be done. Neither liked themselves in their new roles. Harry had become a tyrant in spite of himself, and Harriet was so meek and mild that she was no more than a cipher. They knew they couldn't go on like this. It was sapping energy from both of them, and neither was giving the other room to grow. Harry turned to self-help paperbacks; Harriet went to support groups and took Assertiveness Training. Once their consciousness was raised, they clearly understood the changes they needed to make in order to go back to living the fullest life possible.

Harriet needed to believe in herself and be more assertive; Harry needed to learn not to be so gruff and to stop acting so superior and know-it-all. Harriet learned that she too quickly gave in and stepped aside when Harry raised his voice; fortunately, Harriet realized that you don't trade years of being put down yourself by putting down another. She knew that, deep down inside, Harry was a kind man who only acted rough because he had been brought up that way; he didn't know he had any options. It would be just as cruel to blame Harry for years of dominance as it would be to fault Harriet for years of laying back. She also knew that his contributions were necessary to their union, his practicality an important ingredient in any imaginative plan of theirs. Harriet's ideas were good, but they were unformed; she needed Harry's help to make them happen.

As for Harry, slowly the realization hit him that he had not valued Harriet for all the contributions she made to their lives, for the peace she brought, for her energy, for her playfulness and spontaneity. If not for her, they would never try anything new. Now that he thought about it, Harriet had come up with some pretty good ideas, especially at the quiet and close times, when they were riding together in the car or sleeping or taking a shower. He had to give her some credit.

At first it wasn't easy, they were so used to the old ways, but their efforts paid off so handsomely that they were encouraged to keep working at it. Both of them felt freer, more useful, more competent. There was a generosity of spirit about their interactions, a sense of mutual pride in a job well done; they were collaborators instead of competitors. Harriet's creative ideas were enhanced by Harry's plotting and planning to make them happen, and Harry's penchant for perfection got plenty of new material to work on. Both admitted that they were richer for this new unity, having enhanced their respective skills through repeated use and the glow of appreciation.

Their relationship got the old spark back. No longer did Harry have to tough it out and carry the load by himself; no longer did Harriet slink away holding in her feelings and dreams. He recognized the fullness of his own powers when used in the right way, not pushy or superior but helpful and kind; she blossomed under his appreciation of her contribution to their relationship and his excellent guidance as her friend. And the whole was greater than the sum of the parts. Harriet was still a dreamer and had no concept of time, and there were occasions when Harry got impatient with her and raised his voice a little, but now they both could laugh at it and move on. More and more, Harry started listening to Harriet's dreams and planning the logical steps to make those dreams reality. Harriet loved him for it, and he loved her in return for her imagination and sensitivity. There was harmony and happiness and new life in their relationship. Now they were a team; hand in hand they faced all challenges—and were equal to the task. Together, they made dreams happen.

It was lovely.

Moral of the story: Two heads are better than one, which is to say, one head is better than half.

CHAPTER 4

Rumination: Daydreaming and Nightdreaming

Biting my truant pen
  Beating myself for spite—
"Fool!" said my Muse to me
  "Look in thy heart and write."

—Sir Philip Sidney

In chapter 1, I mentioned Dr. James Asher and his work with the comprehension method of foreign language study. I spoke of the grace period of a "silent time"—a time of inner learning, assimilating, ruminating—last granted to us when we were eighteen months old and learning our mother tongue. That was the last time that anyone rejoiced in a performance approximately right. Even coming close to saying "milkie" or "blankie" was a cause for great celebration then— and gave us milk or blankets. What power! And what fast learners we were in that supportive atmosphere. From that point on, whatever we learned had to be demonstrated with proficiency at once.

We need to reinstate the important "silent time" in our writing process, at the prewriting or rumination stage. We call it daydreaming, or we say our mind is "drifting off," when in fact it is not drifting off but engaged and making an important contribution to our writing. We need to recognize and even invite the prewriting or incubation period, to designate a Rumination Chair or perform a repetitive, familiar task (jogging, taking a shower, driving in the car). Invite the daydreaming and distractions that will help your final idea gel.

JORDAN AND "SILENT TIME"

The story of Jordan illustrates the principle of silent time—what happens when we let things go in the natural way, without forcing production. Jordan was six years old, and already he hated to write. While his first-grade classmates scribbled away, he tore the paper with his pencil, digging deep slashes in anger. I thought it might be his frustration with forming letters and thinking about words at the same time—in chapter 1 we talked about the enormous pressure on a little one just beginning to write, as he forms letters and ideas simultaneously. So I would sit with Jordan and tell him that he did not have to write out his ideas, just dictate them to me and I would write them for him. "No!" He pulled away the pencil that was cutting grooves into the desk. "How about no story, but a list of wonderful words?" I took a sheet of paper and wrote "Jordan's Wonderful Words" in big letters across the top. "Just tell me words that you like, and I will write them down." Silence. "How about *phosphorescence*? That's a word Emily Dickinson liked." Silence. I wrote down *phosphorescence*.

This went on for several weeks. Now I was the one feeling frustrated. What could I do to reach this kid? Why did I think that my assignment, in teaching this first-grade class, was to capture and hold the power over words that they already felt? Who would have thought that a six-year-old would have writer's block? I tried every ploy I could think of, but I could not get Jordan to write.

Now, when you are an adult who hates to write, you turn your anger and frustration inward; six-year-olds annoy their neighbors. I finally told Jordan that he could stay in class on one condition: he was not allowed to bug the kid sitting next to him. He didn't have to write. He could walk around the room, he could sit in a corner and read, he could draw or color. The only rule was, he was not allowed to hit, pinch, or distract the other children.

This arrangement went on for seven months. Every once in awhile, I would make an overture and be rejected. I tried everything. I brought in unusual objects to touch and talk about; we danced to music; we looked at pictures. Nothing. Jordan would not write. Not even a word. Finally, I let go. I stopped trying to cajole him, to amuse him. I let him be. As long as he wasn't bothering the others, he could stay in class. That was it. Soon I forgot he was even in the room and just went ahead and worked with the other children. Several more months passed. We put together a little book, a compilation of the class stories. Jordan had no entries.

I took the whole class to see Shakespeare's *The Tempest*. When we came back, they wrote wonderful stories about Caliban ("Caliban was mean. He was a monster. He never brushed his teeth. He had no friends") and Ariel ("Ariel was sweet. She"—they always thought that Ariel was a she—"writes thank-you notes whenever she gets a present"). We talked about similes and comparisons, and they came up with analogies that were fresh and picturesque. Jordan wrote nothing. We talked about sound, listened to noises, and wrote poems about sound. We talked about alliteration and came out with strings of words that sounded musical. All this time, nothing.

Then one day it happened. I asked Jordan if he would like to dictate a story to me and I would write it down. At first he said no, but then he relented. Haltingly, he said some words, and I printed them on his paper in big letters. Suddenly, he grabbed the pencil out of my hand and started to write furiously. To my astonishment, he wrote in cursive. I didn't even know that he knew how to print—I thought that that was part of his problem. But there he was, writing up a storm, and he was writing in longhand. And guess what? Everything was in there. Similes, sounds, alliteration—even Caliban and Ariel. Everything that we had talked about in class. He *had* been paying attention. Who would have guessed it?

"Jordan!" I said. "That must be a magic pencil! You brought a magic pencil to school today!" He looked a little sheepish, but he was grinning. "She thinks it's magic," he said to his regular teacher. "It's not magic."

A dam had broken loose. Jordan was now able to write fluently and wonderfully. All that time that he walked around or read, he was actually working. He was taking in information, without having to produce anything. When he was ready to produce, he was way ahead of the rest of the class, who had been writing every week for ten months. He had been allowed the luxury of a silent time, a time of assimilation. All that time, he was learning, actually learning more, and more deeply, than he would have had he been forced to produce.

Now Jordan is the best writer in the class. In fact, one of his stories was accepted to publication in *Cricket*, a national children's magazine.

There is a little bit of Jordan in each of us. Only you know how much time you need. Forcing yourself to produce before you are ready guarantees turgid prose. What we call procrastination might well be incubation, and the importance of prewriting—sorting things through, assimilating, making connections—has rarely been recognized or allowed in our schools. Remember the baby learning to speak. All of that mind mapping, syntax building, connecting and sounding out, all of that going on inside her head well before she started to articulate—the comprehension stage came first, before production. With all other learning, especially with learning to write, comprehension and production are expected simultaneously.

WRITING ON THE RIGHT

In order to do your best writing, you need to allow the right brain to make a contribution to your work. Learn to recognize the times that Ariel sends you messages, and be open to those contributions. Once you are aware of them, capitalize on those occasions and even stage them.

Do you get a lot of good ideas in the shower? What! and you go in there without an underwater pen? How about when you are jogging or driving along a familiar route? You know the times: your brain is on automatic, and suddenly you see the stars. Where are your pen and paper? Francis Bacon, the sixteenth-century philosopher, knew that you should never be without a writing utensil. Said Bacon:

A man would do well to carry a pencil in his pocket and write down the thoughts of the moment. Those that come unsought are commonly the most valuable, and should be secured, because they seldom return.

Now you know. The treatise *Of Discourse* was written on the run.

How many times have you been presented with just the right words while you were driving the car—a great idea for your opening line, the perfect conclusion, the ultimate theme that ties up your grand plan—and then thought, cockily, "Well, I will just write that down as soon as I get to the office"? Unh unh unh. Write it down right away!

EXERCISE 4: SIMUL-DRIVE

Sit up straight at your desk and stare ahead. Raise your left hand to grip an imaginary steering wheel. Put a pad of paper slightly to your right and a pen or pencil in your hand. Keep your eyes on the road, make a car noise if you like, and, without looking at the paper, write on your pad, "I know I will not be able to read this." Take a moment right now and do that for yourself. Do not attempt to dot the i's or cross the t's.

You will be amazed at the legibility of your scratching. Remember, in any gathering of words of this sort, what you are after is recalling the key word or phrase that pulls it together. That's what you need to record. That one word will bring back all the rest of your inspiration.

A PERFECT PEN FOR EVERY PLACE

I have a collection of zany pens and pencils, all of which are designed to help the writer capture the elusive unsought word. They include a pen that peels out paper from its cap (excellent for joggers), a pen that lights in the dark (particularly useful for early morning writing or when driving through dark tunnels), and a pen designed by NASA to write in extremes of temperature, in any direction, under water and over butter. A pencil that always gets a pleased response is my wooden spoon pencil, which is indispensable for those of you who get great ideas while cooking.

All of these tools have one thing in common: their purpose is to remind you that the ideas that come at unplanned moments are frequently worth saving, and if you equip yourself with a tool for netting these ideas, you will be rewarded in your pursuit. A handy pen will help you take full advantage of those times when Ariel's flights of fancy have full rein and Caliban is mostly asleep. You will be astonished to see how useful the thoughts you capture in these unconventional writing moments will be to your final product.

Contrary to popular opinion, you *can* perambulate and masticate simultaneously (otherwise known as walking and chewing gum)—and it follows that you can also ruminate while you peregrinate. Armed with the perfect writing utensil for every purpose, you will soon find your ramblings peripatetic as well as poetic.

I trust you hear what I am saying: incorporate these times into your writing pattern. Welcome and seek the contributions that Ariel makes, and tell Caliban to bug off and come back later. It's just you and Ariel and your NASA pen, telling all the world what is nearest and dearest to you and expressing it in your finest way.

The truth is that we usually fight the contributions of this twilight zone part of us; we don't acknowledge them by recording them and giving them credit. I am asking you instead not only to welcome such ideas but to invite them as well—go out of your way to make them happen, and be sure you always have paper and pen within easy grab. The very act of equipping yourself is a guarantee that ideas will come to you. Carrying a writing tool with you wherever you go is guaranteed to send the message to your brain that you are receptive to ideas. And, once you start attending to it, the experiences multiply.

DELIBERATE STAGING

Once you recognize the value of the words that come to you unsought from the right hemisphere across the corpus callosum at idle moments, you will see that I am not being flip to suggest deliberately staging such moments. If your creative well has dried up, go for a walk, take a shower, drive around the block—allow yourself some reflective time. And bring a pad and a pen with you.

Acknowledge that this musing is actually part of the writing process, a kind of prewriting that is integral and necessary to the finished product. Allow time for this preliminary plateau when you schedule your writing.

THE EVA SHER MEMORIAL RUMINATING CHAIR

In fact, I believe so strongly in the importance of prewriting, or rumination, that I want you to set up two separate chairs in your workspace. Designate one the Writing Chair, and the other the Ruminating Chair. If you do not have the luxury of two chairs, simply designate two different directions for the same chair; pull out the side slide in your desk for ruminating, and face front for writing.

It is not a matter of "drifting off" and then "getting back to business"—both operations engage your mind in different ways. Setting up a Ruminating Chair is an acknowledgment of that fact.

Marilee Zdenek notes, in her book *The Right-Brain Experience*, that little girls who stared out the window got in trouble, while the ones who "applied themselves" got good grades. So we treat our brains like little girls at school. We send mental disciplinary notes home when we catch ourselves using the right side of the brain. Rather than inviting rumination, we chastise ourselves for it.

The Ruminating Chair, on the other hand, allows you to honor both reflection and work. When you find yourself musing, turn to the desk slide or get up and move to the Ruminating Chair. When you are ready to write, move back to your Writing Chair, or turn toward your writing position.

The "Eva Sher Memorial Ruminating Chair" was named after a lovely person who found that allowing herself time to ruminate was a key to her new productivity. Eva, let me explain, is the mother of three small children. She has plenty of talent and precious little time. Her husband, Ron, good-naturedly offered to take the children on Saturdays so she could write in peace and quiet. Sometimes when he came back after a harried day of three little ones tugging at him, he—understandably—wanted to know what she had produced. Eva felt terrible if she had nothing to show. She felt pressured to produce pages and pages of material to justify a day of writing work.

When I introduced Eva to the idea of the Ruminating Chair, her eyes lit up. She immediately recognized its value and its importance to her writing, an importance that she had been denying. She set up a Ruminating Chair in the family den at once. Now when Ron returned, she could say proudly, "Ah! I have been ruminating!" (This sounds especially effective when you roll the r with a bit of Scottish flourish.)

And as soon as Eva let go and recognized that rumination too was work and part of the process, the next time she sat down to write, she was able to go to her Writing Chair and produce volumes of quality stuff. She had simply allowed herself to incorporate rumination into her writing work flow.

The truth is that musing is just as much work as the writing itself, and it deserves to be accepted as part of the process.

THE ART OF STARING OUT THE WINDOW

"Something beautiful is forever a joy."

The story is told that John Keats first began his long poem *Endymion* with this less-than-gripping line. He then stared out the window awhile rearranging the words to finally click with "A thing of beauty is a joy forever." Prof. Cosmos Fishawk is in the company of Keats when he comes back with his snappy rejoinder to his left-brained nephew, Skyler.

Deliberation rumination—staring out the window, otherwise inviting and encouraging that important prewriting period, and recognizing it as part of the *process*—cuts down on deadly premature editing, the too-early interference of left-brain logic with right-brain writing.

When I am working with young authors, we often spend forty-five minutes of the allotted hour talking about the stories, drawing pictures, listening to music—and only fifteen minutes writing. And what writing!! One first-grade class I work with once a week "published" three fifty-page books in one year.

So whenever you're lost for ideas, don't be afraid to stare out the window or move to your Rumination Chair for inspiration.

And don't call it procrastination. Call it incubation—it's part of the process.

PAY ATTENTION TO YOUR DREAMS

The authors of *Superlearning* tell the story of Elias Howe, the inventor of the sewing machine. He had worked out all the intricacies of his clever machine, but one part stumped him: he couldn't figure out how to connect needle and fabric. He went to fitful sleep, tossing and turning in his anxiety. He dreamt that he had been captured by spear-waving cannibals, who were shouting and dancing around him, ready to boil him in a big black cauldron. Just when he thought he would pass out from the sheer horror of it all, he looked up and noticed that the spears had holes in their tips. He awoke with a start and realized that all he needed to do was put the needle hole at the tip of the needle to get the sewing machine to work.

Dorothy Brande, in her classic *Becoming a Writer,* details a surefire way to write while the left brain is quiet. It sounds painful, and I personally avoided it for years. Finally, I succumbed, and the results were dramatic. In fact, using the technique described below is exactly how I wrote a large portion of this book.

EXERCISE 5: REVEILLE! REVEILLE!

Ms. Brande suggests that, whatever your normal rising time, you get up a half or even a full hour earlier. (I can hear the groans already; please read on.) As soon as you get up, start to write. Write without reading, without having a cup of coffee, without stopping to reread what you have written—simply write. Write whatever comes into your head; write that this is a foolish assignment at best and an excruciating one at worst. Write that you see no purpose in this, or write the paper or memo or letter you had been putting off writing.

When I first started following Brande's advice, my words were quite hostile. I wrote things like "I simply can't believe that my brain is engaged at this hour of the morning without coffee." I resisted and resisted and finally gave in to the sheer evidence that I was writing more in less time than ever before in my life.

The return on your dawn investment is geometric rather than arithmetic. The work that you do during your reverie writing multiplies itself throughout the day. It works like a self-cleaning oven; once you have set it, you do not even have to be in the same room with it—it grinds away, doing all the dirty work for you. When you start your day by writing, the rhythm and the assignment stay with you all day, even if you don't get back to the project. By the next morning, your output is dramatically increased. You will find that, when you rise again to write, you have at your fingertips more than double, often triple, the amount of output of the day before. Your writing will have an energy and flow that not only picks up on the work of the day before but also somehow incorporates all the mental, possibly unconscious musing of the twenty-four hours in between. Before you know it, the piece you have been putting off is finished.

There is a reason why you don't reread what you have written, read any other material, talk to anybody, make a pot of coffee, or do whatever else you usually do in the morning to get yourself going, get your brain in gear. That's the point exactly. You do not *want* your brain to be in gear. You want the left side of your brain to "refuse to process" the writing that you do at this hour. That way, you are free to capture what Brande calls your own "internal hum." You are free to experience what it is like to write on the right side of the brain.

▶ **Progress Log:** Make an entry in your Progress Log regarding your experience with early morning writing.

HOW TO MAKE A WRITING WORKSHOP HUM

When I am giving a two-day writing workshop, the first night I challenge my students to get up the next morning before class and write in this way. I quote (or blame) Dorothea Brande, tell them about the internal hum, and promise that the room will be humming the next morning if they all agree to do it.

And it is absolutely true; a special spirit is created in the room the following morning, and there is a big smile (a kind of secret smile) on each person's face as he or she walks into the room. Hummmmmmmm. Hummmmmmmm. The hum is almost audible. These people have given themselves a gift, and they feel happy about that, but it is much more of a gift than they at first realize. It is not simply that they were able to write; most of them report, with no little surprise, that the exercise was fun. What *most* pleased and surprised them is what came out. This is exactly what Donald Murray, innovative and candid teacher of writing at New Hampshire University, is talking about when he speaks of the "moments of surprise" that are integral to any writing worth reading.

Most important, what the workshop participants have given themselves is an experience of writing without thinking. ("Forget," says Brande, "that you have any critical faculty at all.") It is not the amount of writing they do or even its quality—what they write in the morning may indeed be gibberish. But the experience of separating the editing voice from the idea creator gives them a power over words that they can call up at will. The point of including this exercise in a workshop is not only to generate the hum, establish community and caring, and get some words down on paper, BUT TO GIVE AN EXPERIENCE OF THE SEPARATION, a mental shift that can be created later, making the workshop a microcosm of what can happen at the workplace.

The results are dramatic. The engine is humming and revved up when I walk in for day two. The whole class is open to the exercises that we do that day and eager to discover even more.

And the same thing can happen for you, in the private workshop of your own mind.

LETTING THE LEFT IN, TOO

If you would like to have the left side of your brain play a part in this multiplicity (remembering that our goal is to be whole-brained), then consider this addition. First, you consciously work out the best approach to the early morning writing you plan to do, then you let your sleeping subconscious go to work on it.

Before retiring, check over the material at hand, look at your outline, pose a question or write a headline, and then go to bed. Actually write that question or headline down in the journal or pad you keep by your bedside. Repeat the question, or the key topic, to yourself several times as you drift off to sleep. When you get up in the morning, all you need to do is to begin entering data around that very topic, without rereading what you have already written or trying to figure out what comes next.

It is like laying out your clothes the night before. Without even thinking, without making any conscious choices, you jump into your clothes, and you're on your way.

IN SUM

I once heard the composer Alan Hovhaness interviewed, the commentary interspersed with strands of his haunting music. One thing that he said struck me particularly. He mentioned that he always carries a little pad with him, and he writes down snatches of music wherever he goes—on the bus, on the street, while waiting for his wife, in the dentist's office—sometimes just a few notes, sometimes entire compositions. It seems very natural that a musician should have music playing in his head. So, too, the writer has words playing. And the words are not just words, just as Hovhaness's notes are not isolated notes. Your words have a pattern and a rhythm, a style and a flow, that is uniquely yours. Capturing that distinctive voice makes your words come alive and distinguishes your piece from any other; that is what makes the reader hear a person behind the words, not a machine. It is that aspect of your writing that ultimately persuades, which is what all writing is about, to one degree or another.

Early morning writing, writing on the run, writing while cooking or driving or showering, the bits that you write when, as Brande says, your "subconscious is in its ascendancy"—all of these, when added later to the edited parts, give your work an authentic ring and make the piece come alive.

Learn to listen to the contributions of your right hemisphere, your Ariel voice. Learn to talk back to the left, the Caliban side, when it offers advice prematurely. Get out all the good parts on paper, and then invite the editorial voice back, at your discretion, to help with structure and grammar and polish. *Separate the two functions when you are writing.* Remember this principle, and you will write well at will.

CHAPTER 5

Branching: The Whole-Brained Way to Organize Your Material

Yes, I will be thy priest, and build a fane
In some untrodden region of my mind,
Where branched thoughts, new grown with pleasant pain,
Instead of pines shall murmur in the wind.
—JOHN KEATS, "ODE TO PSYCHE"

Now that you have got all these words on paper, you need some structure. Many, if not most, writing instructors insist that you prepare an outline before you write. Since the majority of them mean a linear outline, you are doomed before you start. The very problems that plague you in getting words on paper will impede the fluency of your ideas as you outline.

Chances are, when your third-grade teacher taught outlining, she taught you the left-brained, linear way to organize your material.

A linear outline is, by its nature, sequential: B follows A; II follows I. The most important rule to remember is that you cannot indicate a division of ideas unless you have at least two of a kind, so you are not allowed to have an (a.) without a (b.) or an (i.) without a (ii.). Bowing to that rule, the linear outline looks something like this:

I. First main idea
  A. Division of that
    a. Subset
    b. Subset
    c. Subset
  B.Division of that
    a. Subset
    b. Subset
    c. Subset

II. Second main idea
  A. Division of that
    a. Subset
    b. Subset
    c. Subset
  B. Division of that

Looks neat, eh? But, as Tony Buzan points out in *Use Both Sides of Your Brain*, what is pictorially neat may be organizationally "messy." Just because it looks smart does not mean that it is smart.

In fact, one of the only virtues of linear outlining is that it looks neat, and that very virtue is its downfall. By working hard to make sure the outline is neat, we effectively cut off any additions or insertions, any new idea. After all, we do not want to mess up our neat outline. When we move sequentially in the world of ideas, we proceed to the next concept under the assumption that we are finished with the idea before it. The fallacy of this method is believing that the concepts we leave behind have been thoroughly thought out and need no extension.

OUTLINES ARE OUT! BRANCH OUT INSTEAD

Branching, on the other hand, which starts from the center and radiates outward, in an expansive approach to organizing material. By its very nature, it allows you to retrace your steps for easy additions and afterthoughts. And often the afterthoughts are the most valuable aspects.

Branching is the classic rejoinder to the school of writing that instructs you to "begin at the beginning, go on until you come to the end and then stop." Branching begins in the middle, goes back to the start and on to the end, and then moves back to the middle again. The process physically begins in the middle of the page, then juts out ideas in outrageous random fashion into a pattern that is not apparent until the exercise is done. The organization of ideas comes from internal logic; it grows out of the ideas themselves. Rather than being imposed from the outside (like pushing round ideas into square boxes), it allows the idea to dictate the form, instead of forcing the form to dictate the idea.

Without question, branching—the principle of radiating out ideas from a central matrix rather than marching them along in linear fashion—increases fluency. Tony Buzan includes in his book detailed examples of what he calls "brain patterning" or "mind mapping." He avers that Oxford University students, when given the chance to outline their test responses in this way, received higher grades working three times faster. He tells poignant stories of children who had been dismissed as slow learners but were judged to be in the genius class when given the opportunity to express their ideas in a pattern radiating outward. Buzan concludes that it is often not the students but the way we have forced them to express themselves that is the problem.

A linear outline is one-sided and left-brained. Branching is multifaceted and whole-brained. Branching gives a picture and encourages

spontaneity (right); at the same time, it provides structure and indi-
cates logic (left).

EXERCISE 6: YOUR TURN AT BRANCHING

Some suggestions on proceeding (not to be mistaken as rules and
regulations):

Begin with a circle or an oval in the middle of your page. It is
helpful if all the ideas radiate off this one central point, to show their
relationship to the main idea.

Stop for just a moment and consider the main point you want to get
across to your readers in the writing task at hand—the purpose of the
letter, the reason for the memo, the key concept of the proposal. Write
that idea, or a single word epitomizing that central theme, in the center
oval, or draw a picture representing it, if you prefer. That is the last
"conscious" thinking that you do.

Branch out *for a minimum of ten minutes*, including even absurd and
silly ideas.

Turn the paper as you go, inserting ideas as they occur to you. Do
not worry about structure or form. Do not impose a pattern; let the
pattern emerge from the material itself.

As an example, here is what a branched outline of this chapter
would look like:

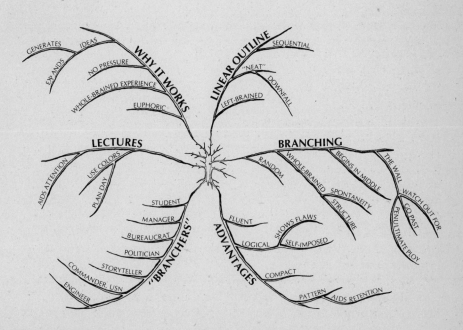

Now, take a fresh sheet of paper, draw an oval or a picture in the middle of the page, set a timer for ten minutes, and begin.

Later, you can go back and group key ideas with colors or dotted-line fences; you can use arrows and put little pictures on the branches, if you like.[1]

Like brainstorming, branching invites you to generate ideas but suspend judgment. As soon as you stop to evaluate an idea or to figure out its place (when you "notice your pen or pencil dithering over the page," as Buzan puts it), then you have lost its cardinal attribute. Get all the ideas out: worry about sense and place after. You will be pleasantly astonished to see how many of these logistical concerns take care of themselves.

The same wall that inhibits rapidwriting operates in branching. This is why you need to branch for a minimum of ten minutes. Just when you think you have run out of ideas, jut out one more line, even though you have no conscious idea of what goes on the end of it. Often by the time you finish drawing the line, the unknown idea is ready and waiting—one you might otherwise have lost out on.

If an idea does not appear, use what I call the Penultimate Ploy. Leave the line going nowhere blank, jut out another line, and put your *next* idea on the following line. The one blocking you is your next-to-the-last idea anyway (the wall! the wall!), and the real gem is just beyond it. Providing a line for the penultimate idea, and leaving it blank, frees you to scale the wall and move on to the better idea beyond.

That is why many of my own branching diagrams include an empty, dangling line. It was a ploy to get on to the best and last idea.

▶ **Progress Log:** Make an entry. What was the branching experience like for you?

ADVANTAGES TO SPIRAL THINKING

The advantages of branching will become increasingly evident the more you use this technique and let its fluent nature generate ideas for you. For one thing, it operates by profusion, inviting new ideas in that abundance. A pleasant sense of discovery and delight often accompanies this method.

For another, branching reveals any flaws in your logic. Sometimes I even use it in reverse as an editing device, when a paragraph or a whole piece is not working. When you put already formulated ideas back into this wheel-and-spoke design, the lapses in logic jump right out at you, allowing you to easily reconstruct the argument from the evidence in front of you.

Another advantage of branching is its compactness. My writing workshop, for example, is ten hours long; I can give an overview of the entire two-day session in one page of branching. Any large-scale writing project (a book, for example, or a long proposal) benefits from this holistic vantage point. What might take six to seven pages of linear outline and lose the relationship of the main points to one another can be done in one page and be kept right beside you as you work. I know authors who have written entire books working from a single sheet of paper.

Branching aids recall and retention, whether you use it to generate your own ideas or to follow the path of another's thoughts. It keeps you alert and attentive, and it creates a kind of positive energy that gives life to whatever work you are doing.

Interestingly enough, branching incorporates all four of the criteria used to evaluate gifted children in creative thinking skills: fluency, flexibility, originality, and elaboration.

PEOPLE I KNOW WHO CALL THEMSELVES BRANCHERS

Men and women and children, too, who take my classes continually amaze me with the new applications they invent for branching. Some of their uses might create connections for you. Feel free to expand on their ideas or create a few of your own.

Clarice, at the Seattle Building and Land Department, uses it to review material. After she reads a chapter of a book or each section of a report, for example, she branches out all the information she remembers. It helps to locate at once the areas that are spotty for her, the pages she needs to go back over. By branching immediately after reading, she locks key concepts in her mind.

K.C., a high school student, used branching to help fill out her college application forms. All that linear fill-in-the-blanks stuff was quite overwhelming her, cutting off the flow of what to include. Inspiration was at a low point, which only increased her anxiety. With branching, she remembered to include some aspects of her accomplishments and goals that she would not have considered otherwise. Then she went back and transposed the information about herself into the linear form that was expected of her. (P.S. She was accepted at the college of her choice.)

Lois is a politician. She is often called upon to give speeches. Ten minutes before her appearance, she branches out on an index card all the points she needs to cover. Then, working directly from the card, she can get up in front of the group and give her speech without the distraction of flipping through pages.

Bob is the Western regional manager of a large shipping company. He used a kind of incremental branching to plot out and get the most benefit from his annual visit to the corporate office in New York by helping him track whom to see and what to say there. Two weeks before leaving, he bought a small pocket notebook and established a separate branching diagram for each executive officer he needed to confer with. As questions came to him surrounding the visit, he added branches on the pages appropriate to the person in charge. He kept linear notes on the blank pages facing. Time was at a premium; he had much to cover and many people to see. The economy of the branched page was exactly what he needed to keep him on target. Later, in discussion with one manager, he might be given another person's name to find out certain vital information; he quickly added another line on the established page. After each meeting, he spent several minutes recapping what he had learned by writing again on the same page with his original branching. When he came back, he had all the information he needed. He told me with a big grin that it was the most productive trip back East he had ever had.

Emily likes to tell stories in front of her class (she is in the third grade). She rehearses for her performances by branching all the key words and the descriptive phrases in her recital. With a picture of her own branching in her head, she does not miss a beat.

Bill is an engineer and a computer whiz who started a class to teach teenagers the basis of computer operation. He needed to know how to distill his vast technical knowledge into something they could grasp and use—which points to stress, what to cover, and what to leave out. In ten minutes of branching, he organized an entire twelve-week class.

Several months later, Bill wrote to tell me that he had written a highly technical book, eleven chapters long, for in-company distribution, and that he had used branching exclusively to build it up. "I found that as I branched out, the material was more logically arranged in my mind, and I typed a pretty good first draft right from the diagram. I branched out for each chapter as well as for the whole work, which collected my thoughts and separated major ideas. The beauty of it was that I had what would have been many pages of linear outline on one page in front of me and could get an overall view." Bill was particularly gratified to learn that the final report was appreciated and understood by people who usually do not read such technical writing, and he credits the pattern provided by his original branching for that lucidity.

Vincent used branching in the waiting room of his therapist. The central theme in the middle of the blob was what he wanted to cover in that session. Then he jutted out all the things that were bugging him, the struggles he wanted to talk about. As his pen ran in circles around and across the page, he started getting insights into his problems, and he saw connections readily that had not been apparent to him before this. He amazed himself at the stuff that he included, at what came out. Then, when it was time for his appointment, he went in and handed the sheet to his therapist. The result was an extremely satisfying and productive session, and he claims that by consistently using this as a tool thereafter, he considerably shortened his treatment.

Jim is a commander in the U.S. Navy. With seven other military leaders, he planned an entire two-week operation on a blackboard using branching. The way he described it, they formed a "collective brain," putting together every aspect of this major undertaking. As they finished a particular phase, a yeoman in the front of the room would copy down the branched diagram from the board and run it off on the copy machine to distribute. Then they would erase the board and go on to the next phase. All was smooth sailing, with a "fair wind and a following sea," and Jim was astonished by the positive energy and crackling of ideas in the room. What might have taken several lengthy and tense meetings was accomplished in one energized one.

LISTENING TO LECTURES IN A NEW WAY, WITH ATTENDANCE

You can use branching to take notes at a lecture. The technique will aid recall immensely, and it will keep you alert and attentive to the speaker. As an instant side benefit, it will make immediately obvious any flaws in the lecturer's presentation. If there are points left undeveloped or irrelevant theses dragged in, you will have the evidence right in front of you.

Attending a week-long conference on learning, I used branching exclusively to record salient points of the presenters' speeches. I was able to retain the best ideas of each presentation on a single page, even for the lectures that were three hours long. When I went back to my room each night, I branched out all the most useful and relevant concepts that I picked up that day and the uses I might make of them. I was astonished at the insights this method of review gave me and, later, at how many of those ideas continue to serve me well.

I was fortunate enough, early on in that week, to sit down next to the master mindmapper, Tony Buzan himself. He opened on his lap an enviable set of twenty-four Pentel colors and rapidly zigged and zagged with an energy and delight that was contagious. That did it! No more black and white branching for me. I purchased, well, eighteen colors and stepped into a new world. It was like Dorothy passing through to the Land of Oz from her monochromatic Kansas; suddenly, all is rainbow-hued. Now I even plan my day in multicolor every morning; somehow the colors themselves help me to remember my plan even when I do not have the diagram in front of me (Call whom? Let's see, it was in blue. . . . Oh, yes, Tom!). Imagine this day plan in color:

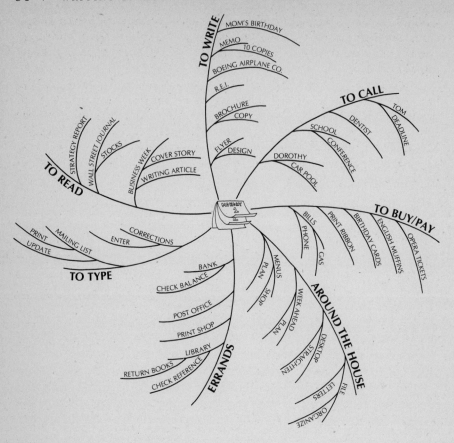

BRANCHING WORKS—SOME REASONS WHY

What fascinates me most about branching is the way it brings out ideas that I know I otherwise would not have thought to include. Sometimes those ideas are "obvious" ones, and I am astonished to see that I had forgotten to consider them before branching; more often, branching invites the special idea, the unique approach, the unconventional, innovative, unexpected addition. It has a way of ferreting out ideas that are hiding in cracks, afraid of the light of day. Perhaps its form looks so playful (especially when you experiment with colors) that ideas let down their resistance to coming forward. Branching also gives you a sense of freedom. It takes the pressure off because you are not locked in; when you move on to a new branch, a new idea, you know that you can always go back. It's like leaving home but knowing your parents did not turn your bedroom over to your little sister—yet.

The most exciting reason of all why branching works is because it is whole-brained; it engages both hemispheres, sending playful and se-rious messages across the corpus callosum simultaneously, which is stimulating and refreshing. You come out of a branching session feel-ing charged up and powerful.

When I give the branching exercise to my classes, people invariably look up smiling after ten minutes. They feel euphoric, and they grin broadly if they have used the Penultimate Ploy to capture yet another idea. They experience feelings of expansiveness, of plenty, of prosper-ity and well-being. This is all true, and it all comes from branching and from the exciting, somewhat heady experience of using both sides of your brain.

CHAPTER 6

Procrastination: Not Just Around but Behind It

When I'm supposed to be writing I clean my apartment, take my clothes to the laundry, get organized, make lists, do the dishes. I would never do a dish unless I had to write.

—FRAN LEBOWITZ

We've put it off long enough. It's time to talk about procrastination.

Procrastination is an ugly, pejorative word. It is a stick to beat yourself with, a kick when you are down. Inherent in the word itself is a moral judgment. The judge and jury have already met. The verdict is passed. You are guilty without appeal.

The cruel irony of procrastination is that it becomes what it sets out to condemn. As soon as we start beating on ourselves for procrastinating, we find ourselves even more lacking in drive, even less motivated to do the writing that needs to be done.

Realizing that you are procrastinating (what! again?) leads to such kick-yourself questions as

Why do I put things off?
Why can't I get started?
Why am I avoiding the inevitable?
Why can't I be like _____ ?
What's the matter with me?

Demoralizing, life-sapping words like *should* and *ought* and *can't* start to reverberate in your head. You find what little energy you had draining away. And you promptly think of several more distractions to keep you from writing.

Procrastination paralyzes and then becomes a self-fulfilling prophecy.

EXERCISE 7: MAKING UP A LIST

Make a list of all the ways you avoid writing. Number your excuses, if you like. Enter the list, complete with the numbering, in your Progress

Log. Do not be modest or chintzy with your entries. The longest list wins a prize.

When we do this exercise in my classes, these are some of the items people come up with:

1. get more paper
2. make a phone call
3. feed the gerbil
4. talk to a plant
5. do more research
6. get another cup of coffee
7. clean out refrigerator
8. rearrange papers on desk
9. start another project
10. get my appointment book up to date
11. sharpen my pencil
12. hope the phone rings

Does your list look anything like that? Good!

Now that you have recognized your inherent creativity in coming up with tactics for avoiding writing, it is time to turn that same creative energy to getting the writing accomplished and, even more significantly, to finding out what is holding you up in the first place.

Procrastination is a form of resistance. Resistance is something we do when we do not feel safe. Find out what it is that makes you feel unsafe, and you will destroy your resistance to writing. Once you understand what is behind your resistance, you are free to make choices.

GETTING TO THE ROOT OF IT

Most advice about procrastination has a major drawback: it treats the symptoms, not the cause. Motivational tricks get you moving again;

enticing rewards act as a carrot on a string, but unless you figure out what made the writing mule balk in the first place, you will not go very far. Maybe there is some danger in the road ahead, some real or imagined reason why the beast has made the decision to stop dead in his tracks. Sure, you might get him going again, but if you have not figured out what he was afraid of, you do not know how to prevent it from happening farther down the road. Soon the carrot trick does not work anymore.

An analogy might be made with diets. There are over two hundred diet books currently on the market, and innumerable spas and clinics are available to help people shed weight. Yet, according to an article in the *Washington Post*, out of every two hundred people who go on a diet, only one loses the weight and keeps it off. The reason, as many psychologists are starting dramatically to realize, is that diets treat the symptom of fat and never address the more fundamental problem of why people overeat in the first place.

Any device—a new pencil, fresh paper, a clean desk—that primes the writing pump will temporarily treat the symptoms of writer's block, just as eating celery sticks instead of hot fudge sundaes will take the pounds off for a week.

But I promised you that I would change the nature of your relationship with writing permanently; in order to do that, you need to get behind the procrastination (not just around it) and find out what is causing it in the first place. That is the only way you will ever be able to change the nature of your relationship with writing permanently. Treat the cause and not the symptoms.

The tricks to get you writing again are a finger in the dike, so to speak. They may save the day—for one day. But the seawall needs major overhaul and repair, and you have only ten fingers. When you run out of digital corks, you will be inundated. (Don't you just love sustained metaphors?) So it is important that you spend some time getting in touch with the cause of the procrastination, the reasons behind it. Only then will you be truly free. Only then you will see that procrastination is a choice, *your* choice: you are not the helpless victim of forces mercilessly outside of you but the one making it all happen. In the immortal words of Pogo, "We have met the enemy and they is us." Once you understand that underlying principle, you will be master of the writing task and no longer at its mercy.

RESISTANCE HAS MEANING

I am *always* leery of absolutes. Myself, I never use them. Like Jane Austen's Edmund Bertram of *Mansfield Park*, "I trust that absolutes have gradations." Yet there is one absolute I will always stand behind. Resistance *always* has meaning. When you find yourself reluctant to act, your body and your mind are trying to tell you something. I want you to take your Progress Log, turn to a clean page, and write this legend in big colorful letters: Resistance *Always* Has Meaning.

Resistance Always Has Meaning

Do it in calligraphy if you like, and put a big, fancy border around it.

The mind and body are so interconnected that even the simple common cold has some meaning in it, if only you will quiet down enough to let it tell you its message. When you delve into the meaning behind whatever it is you are resisting, you will discover that there are choices underlying the work stoppage, a payoff that makes *not* writing somehow more attractive than writing. Maybe your cold is telling you to slow down and take better care of yourself or providing you with a handy excuse not to have guests over. You may be resisting completing a certain writing project because you don't want to face having your boss tear it apart.

The resistance that we speak of here is a different kind of resistance than we talked about earlier when we came up against the wall. There the resistance was a friendly challenge; a word of encouragement was all that was needed—like Beatrix Potter's sparrow telling poor trapped Peter Rabbit, "I implore you to exert yourself"—and wonderful words lay just beyond. Here we are talking about resistance that is hard-core and mean. And it does not pay to fight it. Yet even at the wall you did not use force. It was a kind of yielding, of letting go, that got you past the wall to the grandeur of the summit, not a giving up or a giving in, just giving way. And that yielding is even more important when the resistance is formidable.

FIGHTING RESISTANCE NEVER WORKS

A funny thing happens when you fight resistance. It gets worse. For example, the more you fight a noise, the louder it becomes. The more you *force* yourself to ignore (i.e., resist) the dripping faucet, the barking dog, the snorer beside you, the more the noise amplifies and infuriates you and threatens your sanity.

Do not fight procrastination. When you get into a power struggle, you often lose. Either you become even more paralyzed, incapacitated, helpless, and lethargic or, if you *force* yourself to write, in spite of a negative energy pushing you in the opposite direction, chances are you will produce turgid, plowing prose that is awful to read. If it is readable at all, it is certainly not your best work. When you write with your teeth gritted, what you write grits the teeth of your reader.

On the other hand, if you acknowledge procrastination, you do not need to dramatize it. There is something very profound about recognizing that. It is not just a noticing, it is a letting go. As in the martial art of Aikido, when you give up the power struggle, you actually regain power, because the opposition has lost its hold on you. Seen in this light, conflict of any kind is positive, a dance of energy. Rather than opposing force with force, overcome it by yielding. Move toward the procrastination, move with it. What does it have to tell you?

THE HEADACHE DISAPPEARING ACT

Notice what happens when you have a headache or a backache, or when you are tired from sitting too long at your desk, or when your neck hurts. Most of us try to ignore complaints like these or think about not thinking about them, and then the pain intensifies. Often such aches and pains will go away if you stop for a moment and ask them why they came. Being PRESENT for a moment to your headache or backache, paying attention to it, is often enough to make it go away and stop bugging you. Also, it is useful to know why you had the pain to begin with.

This same approach works well for little children who are interrupting your work. Be PRESENT to your nagging child. Perhaps all the little one wants is a moment of your attention, to touch base, to know you care, and then he or she will let you alone so you can get back to your writing. You can see where this idea is leading. Be PRESENT to your procrastination and not only will it go away but, before going, it will tell you why it was there in the first place.

RELAX AND TAKE THE ONUS OUTUS

So first, *relax*.

"Ah yes, here I am procrastinating again."

Believe it or not, there is no morality here, so take the moral judgment out of it; simply accept your procrastination as a statement of fact. You are not an awful person and there is nothing the matter with you; you are procrastinating, pure and simple.

One way to accept procrastination is to give it credit for being often an important contribution to the writing, a time of incubation (see chapter 4).

Give yourself points for your creativity.

"That is a clever ruse, self. Research is always a noble pursuit. No one could accuse you of sloughing off."

Research is worth at least ten points.

Or, "It was creative of you to think of cleaning your desk right now. No run-of-the-mill excuse here for not facing the pad. After all, who can work with a messy desk?"

That is worth eight points.

Give yourself credit for bring it into awareness.

"I'm glad you brought this diversionary tactic to my attention. This time I was only X minutes into my favorite tactic #X." (Use numbers from the list you created earlier.) Reducing things to a number takes away their power and personality, as we know too well when we ourselves are reduced to a social security or student ID number.

THE PROGRESS LOG COMES INTO PLAY

Now take that conversation with yourself and enter it into your Progress Log. Remember that a log records a journey, and progress implies moving forward—so whatever you enter is good news: you are gathering more useful information about yourself and the ploys you use to keep from writing. Bringing into your awareness actions that were previously outside of your consciousness is the first plateau in regaining control.

Be specific. Enter as data the time of day; the people, if any, involved; the tricks you are using; the piece you are working on; the intended audience; the deadline date; and *how long* you were procrastinating before you brought it into awareness. The bemused, bespectacled anthropologist pose applies here too: record the data without interpretation, without judgment. Let the pattern emerge; do not impose one.

GET BEHIND IT AND FIND OUT WHAT IT MEANS

Now that you have stopped fighting your procrastination, find out what it is telling you about yourself. Often just discovering what is behind the resistance is enough to pull the plug and get you writing again.

In some sense, the whole first half of this book is about procrastination and how to foil its curse: any one of the exercises in other chapters used to promote fluency will also serve you well for breaking through the procrastination barrier and getting at the meaning behind it.

1. Rapidwrite Your Way Out of Procrastination

Use rapidwriting to get at the meaning behind your procrastination. Simply sit down and start to write—not in that forced "I-am-going-to-write-if-it-kills-me" mode, tensely clutching pen or pencil, but by getting your anxieties and reluctance out on paper. Write out how you are putting this project off, and describe what is bothering you about it and why it is not headed in the direction you want. Often the problem solves itself as you write it out. Sometimes rapidwriting helps uncover an anxiety that is outside of the writing project itself yet keeping you off task. Once I found myself wasting a whole morning instead of writing; through rapidwriting, I discovered that it was concern about a sick friend that was causing the distraction. As soon as I had named my concern, I felt relief.

Once you get all that out of your system, you might as well keep on writing, and before you know it, you will have tricked yourself into writing—and writing well!!—the piece that threatened you. If you think your ramblings are going nowhere, be sure to include that judgment, but *keep on writing.* Soon you will have your piece done. Simply edit out the extraneous chatter.

2. The BP Entry

An often dramatic way to get the engine humming once more is to turn to your Progress Log and make a BP (Before Procrastination) entry. This approach works best when a project that has been rolling along suddenly stops cold. Want to get those wheels in motion again? Why did you stop in the first place? Resistance has meaning, and once you know the meaning, you are free to make choices.

Label the entry BP in the margin, and answer these questions:

What was the last paragraph, the last sentence that I wrote?
Where do I go from here?
What happens when I finish this?

Often, the answers you produce will make the situation apparent and clear the air to go back to work. An accountant in one of my courses, for example, was writing to a client, detailing the activity of his investment. He had the first half of the report neatly done and then kept putting off getting back to finish it. A BP entry solved the dilemma: the last paragraph he wrote had been about the good stuff that was happening; the answer to "Where do I go from here?" would contain all the bad news. He went back and reworked the report so that the lines of demarcation were not so rudely drawn.

A graduate student was dragging her feet on finishing her dissertation. The BP entry provided a valuable clue. She actually felt secure and happy in the academic womb, and venturing out into the job market with her new degree terrified her. The answer to "What happens when I finish this?" let her in on her psyche's secret; she lined up a satisfying job first and finished her writing at night, making the transition easier.

3. Branch Your Way Out of the Procrastination Box

You have already seen the usefulness of branching to help pull together ideas and put them in order. One of the astonishing aspects of using this free-flowing approach to organizing your material is the gratifying way it often presents you with ideas that you did not know you had when you first sat down to compose. The same gift occurs when you use branching in a therapeutic way. Branching will help you to get in touch with your writing anxiety.

Why is it that I cannot (or, more correctly, Why is it that I choose not to) write this piece?

Identify the assignment in the center, and branch out everything that bugs you about it, keeping it from speedy completion. Just as fast as you can, jut out all the reasons that make it safer to procrastinate than to begin, or continue, writing. Procrastination is resistance, and resistance is digging your heels in when you are being pushed in a direction where you do not feel safe. What is unsafe about the territory that you fear to tread? Let branching help you ferret out the rascal answers hiding in the closet of your mind. C'mon out, wherever you are, face me like a true opponent, put up your dukes, prepare for battle. Sometimes, when you see the actual size of your anxiety, you will laugh instead of fight—and then get back to your writing.

4. Rise to Write in the Morning

Dorothea Brande's idea of "early morning writing" can provide a powerful breakthrough for prolonged procrastination. It is especially revealing if you pose the question "What is it that is keeping me from finishing this piece?" before retiring. Place a journal or a notebook by your bed and write out your resistance in the morning. Because your brain is not awake enough to provide ready answers, you will be astonished at the insights you receive.

BITE YOUR TONGUE—LEARN TO LISTEN

If you want to learn to listen to yourself, to quiet down your noisy left hemisphere enough that your right can tell you what is happening with your writing, first learn to listen to another human being.

Do you know how to totally listen with your whole heart and full attention to another person? Once you have mastered that talent (it only takes three minutes, so take heart), it is easy to turn those newfound listening skills inward.

In our everyday listening, or what passes for listening in our society, we are so accustomed to supplying answers, interjecting advice, murmuring sympathy, and offering similar tales of woe that we work our mouth muscles more than our ear muscles. A surprising thing happens when we totally listen with our mouths closed. When we give others our undivided concentration, we offer them the opportunity to get in touch with answers inside themselves that are often more appropriate than anything we might supply. In my seminars we do a listening exercise that also models the working vocabulary of a master, the one making the choices. When you do it yourself, you will find that the exercise has several interesting and useful peripheral benefits:

1. It teaches you to listen, showing you how to quiet down enough to hear what another person is saying;
2. It shows dramatically what truths come forth when you give another person the total and complete gift of being listened to;
3. It gives you, in turn, the experience of being listened to and, within that reassuring space, helps you get in touch with your own answers behind your procrastination;
4. It gives you the working vocabulary for changing from a victim to a person in control, making choices, calling the shots;
5. It teaches concretely the power of words in shaping person and personality; and
6. It teaches you, by example, how effective it is to turn these newfound listening skills inward.

All this in four three-minute segments!

EXERCISE 8: LISTENER AND LISTENEE

You will need a partner. One without experience is fine, for he or she will be getting OJT—on-the-job-training. And, of course, you promise to return the favor to the listener—who would begrudge you three minutes of his time knowing that you, in turn, will give him three minutes of yours?

One of you is A and the other B. A is the first to speak, while B listens. I think that it is apt to call B the listener and A the "listenee," for the latter is not just a person speaking but someone being listened to. Perhaps for the first time in her life, another human being is actually giving three full, uninterrupted minutes of time, and complete attention.

Part 1: The Victim Speaks

A, you are in for a treat. I want you to tell B all your worst fears about writing and detail your very best tactics for procrastination. You may refer to writing in general or center your remarks around a particular writing project that you have been avoiding. For three solid minutes, you have the floor and your partner's rapt attention. Since you are coming at this part of the exercise from a victim position, I want you to use the vocabulary of a victim. Incorporate these words and phrases as much as possible into your conversation:

Vocabulary of a Victim

should
ought
can't
it's really not my fault
I'm an awful person

As in "I really should be working on this strategy report. I don't know what's the matter with me. I just can't get started. Every time I set aside some time to write, something else comes up that demands my immediate attention. It's really not my fault. I ought to get up earlier in the morning, or stay up later at night, I suppose, but I work hard all day and all these interruptions keep getting in my way. I can't seem to do anything about it. I guess I'm just an awful person."

Three minutes. And during this time, B listens intently—and says nothing. The only noise that B is allowed to make is an affirmative "uh-huh" or an occasional "Hmmmm. I see what you mean." Bite your tongue before saying anything more.

The B's often get sore tongues during round one.

When we do this exercise in my seminars, the body language is wonderful to watch. No matter how many A and B teams are talking simultaneously, each listener manages to focus totally in on the "listenee" and screen out all the other voices. The person listening leans

forward, totally engrossed; the person talking looks free and somewhat surprised to have the full and undivided attention of another
human being for three full minutes. Together, they make an intent
unit.

Then we switch and let B do the talking, while A follows all the
game rules listed above.

Part 2: The Master Answers

The words we use when we talk to ourselves can actually affect our
beliefs and our behavior. In her wonderful, life-giving book *Celebrate
Yourself,* Dorothy Briggs devotes an entire chapter to the importance
of words in forming our beliefs. She calls this chapter "Watch Your
Language!" and I recommend that you look at it, especially if you
have any doubt in your mind that your choice of vocabulary shapes
who you are and how you perceive yourself.

We are what we say we are. We become self-fulfilled prophecies.

Have you ever seen that plaque "Children Learn What They Live,"
which says, "If a child lives with criticism, he learns to condemn. If a
child lives with praise, he learns to appreciate," and so on? The same
dynamic holds true for the adult and the self-talk that shapes him
daily. In other words, what you think about is what you become. If
you continually use the victim vocabulary, you will see yourself as a
victim and, in fact, live your life that way. Substitute the life-giving
power of words of choice and choosing and your world will expand
with a sense of potential. Change your self-talk and you change yourself. Catch yourself in the act of saying negative brow-beating things
to your own psyche, and purge out the negativism. Substitute a kind
thought for an unkind one. Stop believing the bad, start believing in
the good. Be a goodfinder instead of a faultfinder.

And start noticing that there is a payoff for procrastination, a reason
why not writing is somehow safer than writing. Notice that you are
also paying a price, parallel to the payoff. What would change for you
if you got all your writing done on time? And what is standing in the
way of that?

Here are two examples of the price/payoff parallel:

"It's costing me a lot in terms of frustration and job dissatisfaction
not to do this report on time, but the payoff is that if I don't write it,
or if I hand it in late, then my boss will not have the time to criticize
it."

Or "It's costing me a promotion not to keep on top of all the writing
this job demands, but the payoff is that if I don't get promoted, then
I can stay comfortable at this level and won't have to worry about
increased responsibilities."

Again, A speaks for three minutes. Again, B is only allowed a nod, a grunt, or any other simple cue to say, "I follow you." This time, however, there is a difference. This time the "listenee" (not just a speaker, remember, but, more important, one being listened to) deliberately incorporates the master's vocabulary into his story. "Should" becomes "want" or "choose"; "can't" becomes "choose not to."

Vocabulary of a Master

choose
choice
wish
prefer
responsibility
price
payoff

The Wall Revisited

By the way, when you are doing this exercise, you will find that you come up against the same wall that halted you during rapidwriting and branching, especially when it comes time to say, "Well, the payoff is. . . " Many people find that they (*think* they have) run out of things to say and in fact feel frustrated that the listener is not rescuing them, as they are accustomed. S.O.P. (Standard Operating Procedure). Push past the wall, keep on talking, even if you talk about not knowing what to say. All of a sudden—because you *were not* rescued—blurp! out comes the tremendous insight for which you alone had the key. Light bulbs pop out all over the room as wrinkles disappear from foreheads.

EXERCISE 9: TURNING INWARD

Once you learn how to listen to another, then it is a simple thing to clear a space inside for yourself, where you can allow your own reasons for procrastinating to come to the fore. There is a purpose in your procrastination, a reason why putting off writing seems safer than doing it. And your right brain knows the answer. The same surprising insights inside others that come forward in the quiet spaces of the A and B exercise are inside you, too, and are yours for the asking—and the waiting.

Get into a comfortable position. Close your eyes. Relax. Notice your own breathing. Quieten yourself, as the British say, meaning slow down inside.

Now ask yourself about this project you are procrastinating on, or about your writing procrastination in general, and let your right brain answer. Since the right brain is providing the answer, the solution or insight might very well come in the form of an image or figure rather than in words at first.

When I was preparing chapter 9, on visualization, the image of a sun came to me. That image did not make sense to me, but I stayed with it. Soon, radiating from the sun came concepts like warmth, fire, light, energy, and—a surprise—royalty. After staying with that image for a while, I felt ready to write, and the sun set the tone that I wanted. I never did quite put into words where "royalty" fit, but I had a sense of grandeur, of dignity, of majesty as I wrote that seemed appropriate to the power of the subject.

So do not reject the image, even if it initially does not make sense to you. Stay with it. Ask for more meaning, and wait for the reply. Eugene Gendlin, in his book *Focusing*, explains that at this point most people experience what he calls a "shift," a kind of "aha!" moment when the curtain lifts or the weight seems removed. He goes on to suggest that you "check" that answer. Get verification, a "yes, that's it" sense. You will know when you have it.

▶ **Progress Log:** Make an entry. What's the price and what's the payoff for not writing?

IN SUM

Perhaps you are starting to see that procrastination is not an outside force and you are not a helpless victim. Procrastination comes from resistance inside, and you can make choices. You are not a victim. You are in charge. You can take command of the situation, move forward, and write.

In fact, when you are no longer encumbered by the psychological drain of procrastination, you will be free to do your best and most fluent writing ever.

CHAPTER 7

Assertiveness Training: Dealing with the Caliban Critic

You taught me language; and my profit on't
Is, I know how to curse.
—CALIBAN, SHAKESPEARE'S *THE TEMPEST*

The Greeks have a mythological deity named Momus, the god of mockery and faultfinding. This carping faultfinder is inside each of us, and, especially when it comes to writing, this Critic nags and bothers us and tries to convince us that since we cannot write effectively at all, why even start? Such a Critic convinces through ridicule, sarcasm, and name-calling, eroding our confidence and enveloping our goals in a miasma of inertia.

The Critic I am talking about here is not the rational friend who intercedes when all is said and done, the voice of reason and restraint who helps us edit, who lets us know what needs to be kept and what needs to be cut. No. The Momus Critic is the one who will not let us get started, the one who puts our stomach in knots when we are facing a blank sheet and makes us think of a hundred and one other things we could be doing at the time. The Momus Critic comments caustically on our choice of words and calls us "dumb" and "stupid."

The Momus Critic is a liar.

Learning to deal with that liar, to take away some of its inordinate power, to cope with its destructive dialogue, to stand up for your rights and beliefs, is what this chapter is all about.

HISTORY OF THE CRITIC: WHERE DID HE/SHE/IT/THEY COME FROM?

Where did this critical voice come from, and why does it hold us in sway? Why have we given it so much power? Why do we constantly internalize the Critic's destructive pronouncements and accept at face value its moral judgments?

In *The Origin of Consciousness in the Breakdown of the Bicameral Mind*,

Princeton scholar Julian Jaynes advanced the remarkable theory that early man had no consciousness but rather what Jaynes calls a bicameral mind, "an executive part called a god, and a follower part called man." Early man functioned, in fact, survived, purely through listening to the god-voice within.

The god-voice gave man advice, threatened him, criticized and even mocked him. Sometimes a visual aura accompanied the auditory one, and the god took on the form of an angel, a devil, a relative, or a familiar person. Jaynes suggests that, because of their authority and control, it was virtually impossible to disobey these gods, and in fact he shows linguistically (*obey* comes from the Latin *obedire, ob- + audire*, "to hear, facing toward") that listening to their decrees constituted obedience and belief. Some vestige of that utmost authority and control must surely exist today as we listen to the Critic's voice and passively demur to his admonitions, even as Achilles obeyed the authority of Thetis, and Moses followed Yahweh's command from the burning bush. Jaynes writes:

> How helpless the hearer! And if one belonged to a bicameral culture, where the voices were recognized as at the utmost hierarchy, taught you as gods, kings, majesties that owned you, head, heart, and foot, the omniscient, omnipotent voices that could not be categorized as beneath you, how obedient to them the bicameral man![1]

The residual of that omnipotent god-voice authority functions today as what Harman and Rheingold, in *Higher Creativity*, call "the guardian of the unconscious. . . . the internal censor at the portals of waking consciousness."[2]

This collective historical perspective is mirrored for many of us in our individual experience. Most of us have had some authority figure unwittingly undermine our confidence in writing, usually under the guise of helping. I met a woman named Erin at an out-of-town conference; we had an instant rapport. Soon after returning home, I received a note from her that ended:

> I hope you can excuse my scribbles and overlook any misspl (good going!) miss-spelling. My Grandmother always answered my letters with corrections on my last letter. Then if I was away from home my mother did the same thing. I told my mother that I thought she, at least, should be glad just to get a letter. But I know it's good for me, otherwise I'd never learn.

Your new friend,
Erin

Perhaps somebody well-intentioned but devastating like that was shaping your Inner Critic early on.

NOW THAT IT'S HERE, HOW DO WE DEAL WITH IT?

What can we do about this Inner Critic? How can we silence it, or at least develop a working relationship with it? These are the chief ways:

First, get to know your Critic.

Second, learn to talk back. Transform the parent-child relationship you have with your Critic into an adult-adult relationship. If all else fails, ask it (politely or not so politely) to leave. You can always have it back, on your terms, in your time frame, at your invitation later, to help with editing in a supporting role.

Last, and most dramatically, set up an actual interview, a conversation with your Critic, to get remarkable insights into what makes the Critic tick and how to get a handle on it.

GET TO KNOW YOUR CRITIC

The Critic can be male or female, a group of people, or a made-up character. Usually, but not always, the Critic is based on some real person you knew long ago or who is currently part of your life. Seeing the Critic as a person—getting to know how he looks, how she behaves and sounds, what tricks they use to keep you from writing—will help you to come to grips with this internal persona who holds you back. The more you know about your Critic, the less power your Critic will have over you.

Using some of the techniques from chapter 6, especially the art of deep listening, you can quickly uncover who your Critic is.

When you name something, you own it. It no longer has power over you once you have called it by name. In the biblical account Adam and Eve named the creatures of the new world and in naming them became masters over them. Eugene Gendlin, in *Focusing*, speaks of the ownership, the shift in carrying the burden that happens when you are able to label a feeling. Giving your Critic a name and a face disarms the Critic's power and puts you back in charge.

The central-casting ability of your brain would make a movie director green with envy. If, to make some sense of the Critic persona to you, your psyche needs to go back twenty-five years to a teacher you had in grade school and have not seen since, your brain will readily supply that image as symbol. If it fits better to connect with a boss or spouse, a perfectionist parent, or a sibling from your world today, then that image will be there for you. It is not uncommon to have the Critic appear as nonhuman: gnomes and leprechauns seem especially popular. And sometimes the Critic is a composite picture of several personalities in your life.

Some interesting profiles emerge when people pause for a moment, turn off the spigot of the Critic's negative stream, and ask the Critic to come forward with an identity.

Richard's Critic came masked to their first meeting, and refused to remove the mask.

Vivian's Critic told her his name. It was Bentley, "and is he ever cute—and a good dresser, too!"

Mark insisted his Critic was his friend (the most insidious kind of Critic): "He only wants to protect me from the outside."

Shiela said her Critic looked like her father, while Rory discovered to his amazement, "My Critic is me! Twenty years ago, without a beard!"

Sometimes the Critic turns out to be a host of people. Remember the therapist in chapter 2 who lived her life "as if there were a panel of judges watching and taking notes"? On closer inspection, these black-robed figures turned out to be family members, who collectively constituted her Critic: "grandmothers, uncles, brothers, stepmother."

If the Critic is a composite picture, it is quite okay to give him a fitting name yourself, if he does not supply one, or even be presumptuous enough to change the name if he presents you with one you do not like. After all, who is in charge here?

A lawyer named George recorded his first conversation with his Critic:

George: Who are you?

Critic: Don't you know by now?

George: Don't answer a question with a question. Who are you?

Critic: I am the person you always wanted to be. I'm smarter, and nicer, and I write better than you and unless you can do all the things I can do (and you never can), and write as perfectly as I do, no one will ever really like you.

George: Well, that's a fine mess you've gotten us into this time, Ollie. I think I'll call you Ollie because the image of Oliver Hardy is hardly one that I find intimidating.

Critic: Oh no you don't. Ollie is not smarter, nicer, or better than you are. You should call me James. James Bond. I like that better.

George: Tough shit. You're Ol'ie to me now, and that's who you are going to stay. Besides, the story you are peddling to me is just a crock. It's the story that an Oliver Hardy would have—that you have to do things better so that people will like you, not because there is a joy in doing things as well as you possibly can. You should do things for the love of doing them, not for the approval of others. A true James Bond would know this, but an Oliver Hardy would hide behind his "accomplishments."

No matter what name or face you give your Critic, there seems to be a certain commonality among these creatures of the deep. The Critic's personality is often caustic and sarcastic, and he likes to demean you. Aloof and superior, the Critic has a tendency to talk down to you. She often makes your ears burn and your throat tighten. He makes your heart sink and turns down the brightness control knob on your enthusiasm and expectations. Being cautious (for your own good, you understand), the Critic warns you against being vulnerable, taking risks, getting hurt. Listening to the Critic's advice takes the wind out of your sails; you are dead in the water. The Critic speaks in absolutes and emphasizes the negative. The vocabulary the Critic uses is the victim vocabulary ("should," "can't," "ought," "awful"), and she encourages you to use the same deathly words. The Critic looks for evidence to support your poor opinion of yourself and then hammers you with it. He ignores positive steps you have taken or dismisses them as inconsequential. She expects giant leaps and has little patience with baby steps. He has no regard for small triumphs and wants instant success. She likes to call you names and push your low–self-esteem buttons.

The Critic is not life-giving, energizing, or encouraging.

Don't you think it is time you came to terms?

EXERCISE 10: SAY HELLO TO YOUR CRITIC

This creature has been living inside of you for twenty-odd years or more; I think it is about time you met. Following the listening prescription outlined in the last chapter, get into a comfortable position, close your eyes, and quiet down in whatever way works best for you. Become conscious of your breathing; use your breath as a pump, exhaling tension, inhaling peace and relaxation. Stay in that peaceful and quiet state for awhile, and then, when you feel ready, invite your Critic in for a cup of tea. You just want to see what he looks like, to hear the sound of her voice, to notice what they have to say to you. You just want the figure to come forward and identify itself. Three minutes is quite enough time.

It is better not to go into this exercise with any preconceived notions. Just let the image of your Critic well up inside of you without your conscious mind trying to force or form the image.

TALK BACK!

The simplest way to handle the Critic, one that surprisingly few people give themselves permission to do, is to talk back. It is important to learn a few handy little "bug off" tricks, some fly swatters to have in your back pocket when the pesky drone is keeping you from finishing your writing. You can be genteel, asking him politely to leave, or you can turn rude, if that works more effectively. You can start out nice, and then if she still insists on bugging you, grit your teeth and yell, "Get out! Now!"

If it helps, you can talk about yourself from the safety and distance of the third person. One fellow in my workshop found dealing with his Critic most effective when he simply told the interfering boisterous voice, "Look. Would you leave the kid alone?"

SAY, "THANK YOU FOR SHARING THAT"

Sometimes the singular device of politely stating, "Thank you for sharing that"—and then moving on—is sufficient. The beauty of this approach is that you do not stop to argue the point or try to out-scream the screamer. You acknowledge the Critic and keep on writing. This is known as the Aikido approach.

Our son Peter was ten when I taught him this one simple dismissal of the Critic. Several days later, he was doing a report on Mozart. The assignment was to write 150 words about the Viennese composer. At 103 (count 'em) words, Peter stopped cold. He had run out of things to say. In fact, he was convinced that he had completely exhausted the topic. There was nothing more to say about Mozart and classical composition. Then he remembered that it was his Critic telling him that, and he remembered how to talk back.

"Thank you for sharing that," he said in answer to his Critic telling him he had nothing left to say about Mozart. Then he kept on writing. And writing. And writing. Soon he came running downstairs to my den, gleeful and grinning, waving his paper. He slapped his forehead with the back of his hand, incredulously. "Three hundred—three hundred!—and thirty-eight words!!!! Gosh, I hope I don't get into trouble for writing too much!"

Saying "Thank you for sharing that" acts as a damper when the Critic turns to "Yes, but. . ." whining that leads nowhere and stops everything. When you do not answer back, however, you soon capitulate, as the following story illustrates.

Every summer, I teach a full two-day writing workshop at the university. It is exhausting but exhilarating. I am on my feet lecturing from 9 A.M. to 5 P.M. for two days straight. By 4:00 of the second day, I am on a roll, the class is responding, and we are dancing together. I feel energized. One year, at 4:10, a woman in the front of the room spoke out.

"You must be exhausted!"

"No, actually, I feel great!"

"Yes, but you have been standing on your feet lecturing with animation for two days. Don't your feet hurt?" She clucked sympathetically.

"Honest. No. I feel fine."

"You are amazing. I could never do that, stand on my feet like that for two days and not be frazzled by four."

I was starting to feel a little weak.

"I admire your stamina. Most people would be incoherent by now, ready to collapse."

All of a sudden, I felt like a broken record, winding down into slow motion. I felt plodding and heavy. Every muscle in my body ached. We crawled to the finish line.

If only I had said, "Thank you for sharing that!" and moved right on!

GET TOUGH! BE BRAVE!

The object is to learn to suppress your Critic, at least temporarily (you will never lose the Critic permanently), so you can get on with the business of writing. Tyson, a screenwriter, told me that her Critic was a childlike gremlin that sat on her shoulder, jumping up and down and squawking, ranting and raving and spitting out criticisms as Tyson tried to work. She convinced him to move off her shoulder and down onto the typewriter—and then she pressed the carriage return and rang him off.

Right now you have a monologue inside, a barrage of refuse raining on your brain. You get smaller and smaller as you allow this dump truck to unload on you. Talk back! Pull rank. Julian Jaynes's bicameral man accepted the dictums of the gods unquestioningly; we no longer need to accept the Critic's voice as definitive. I am encouraging you to make that monologue a dialogue, and give a few answers of your own. Do not be intimidated. Call the Critic's bluff. Strip away his puff and thunder. Remember in the *Wizard of Oz* how their knees knocked as Dorothy and her companions entered the Wizard's throne room? ("Please, sir! A heart.") The Wizard seemed so omnipotent and unapproachable. Then Toto pulled down the curtains to reveal a very small man pulling levers and making all kinds of amplified noise.

Of course, the Critic is often present in much that we do, not just writing; learn to transfer over to writing the ways you have learned to deal with him in other arenas. My cousin Mary Edna is a watercolorist of considerable talent. Her Critic tries to sabotage that ability whenever possible. People are startled to hear her carry on an audible conversation with herself as she paints.

"Darker pigment. More magenta. No. Yes. Be brave!"

It is this last rejoinder that gets her through and helps her produce magnificent artwork. "Be brave! Be brave!" That simple injunction gives her the courage to apply more paint, use brighter colors, and not be weak-willed in her brush strokes. I borrowed her phrase for my writing and find it often helps me through a difficult passage. Be brave!

USE DEADLINE ENERGY

Now that you know the Critic and see how listening to his or her voice is killing you, you will no doubt recognize that it is the inability to silence this voice sooner that leads to putting off writing until the last minute.

All of us have had the experience of putting out a piece of dynamite work under pressure—deadline crisis gives us writing adrenaline, and we become like people who lift extraordinary weights during floods. When you or someone you love is in danger, when the flood waters are rising, there is no time to listen to the voice inside that says, "You can't do that!" In a similar way, deadline energy generated by the crisis of the eleventh hour pushes all objections out of the way and clears the road for us to write our best and do it with ease. Out of necessity, we turn off the Critic's voice and write as fast as possible because we believe we have no other choice. The situation is life-threatening, and we respond with our finest hour of writing.

Once I asked some college students, who had just handed in their term papers, what approach they had used to get the papers in on time. One young man shared this: "I went to the movies, then I went to a party, ate lots of pizza, had a few beers, and then came home at midnight and *powered* it out!" (This last wonderful phrase was accompanied by a rrrrrum sound and a gesture of plowing through.)

Without realizing it, he was describing how to use deadline energy to get past the Critic. We let writing go until the last possible moment because we have not trained our minds yet to turn off the Critic's voice under any other circumstances than being clutched.

"Out of my way, I don't have time to listen to you. I've got to get this writing done!"

There is a more positive way to let deadline energy work for you.

How to Work with Deadline Energy

1. Accept it, know that it is your working style, take the moral judgment out of it, and LEAVE SUNDAY NIGHT OPEN.
2. Push it up a week or so earlier to take the frantic pace out by recognizing that the Critic is the culprit. You now have at your disposal any number of less stressful ways to anesthesize the screener, using early morning writing, rapidwriting, answering back, and other devices detailed throughout this book.

Now you have a choice. Recognize why you are waiting until the last minute, or move your deadline up a bit, write just as well, and give yourself a chance to look over what you've written before you submit it.

IT ALL TIES TOGETHER

Already you can discern how coming to grips with the Critic pulls together the work you have been doing throughout the other chapters of this book. After all, the Critic **is**

- Procrastination
- Caliban
- The Premature Edit Mode
- Your third-grade teacher with the red pen
- The left brain
- The wall
- Jon telling Garfield that cats can't walk on their hind feet.

Rapidwriting works because you "power it out" past the Critic. Branching is dramatic because you ease the Critic out of the task. Rumination thwarts her because she meant for it to be harder than that. Early morning writing is fluent because the Critic is still asleep. He needs his sleep, so let him sleep—meantime, you write what you need and want to write. And your Progress Log has already given you insight into some of the Critic's tactics and ploys; by helping you uncover the pattern, it has already started to put you back in control.

INTERVIEW WITH THE CRITIC

Now that you know the Critic's name and phone number and have a trick or two up your sleeve to momentarily distract him, it is time to have a more in-depth conversation, to lay out some ground rules for the new relationship you plan to form. An interview is the best way to do this. It helps to clear the air and gives you a new position—a position of authority and strength. Right now, you have a parent-to-child relationship, and you want to change that. You want to begin to develop an adult-to-adult friendship.

EXERCISE 11: AN INTERVIEW WITH THE CRITIC

Stance

For this first official encounter, a few positions need to be established. You want to get at the Critic's identity and uncover his work habits, his modus operandi. You want to redefine the parent-to-child attitude, and you want to assert yourself and point out that the Critic is standing on your toes. Think of yourself as a journalist on assignment; this distancing helps, especially in the first interview. Recognize that your subject is coming to this interview with a lifetime of pushing you around and getting his own way in everything. He has a reputation for being sullen and sarcastic. We are talking big-time interview here. This is like Oriana Fallaci interviewing the Ayatollah Khomeini. She never let him have the last word. This is serious stuff, and you must not let the Critic get the upper hand.

Questions

Professional interviewers know never to ask yes-or-no questions; instead, they pose questions that need detailed replies. Rather than "Are you happy with this decision?" a good interviewer might ask, "What are some of the things about this decision that please you?" Similarly, in approaching your Critic, do not ask, "Can I get rid of you?" but rather "How can I get rid of you?" or "What are some ways we could improve our working relationship?" Not "Don't you like the way I write?" but "What is it that you don't like about my writing?"

When you formulate your questions, consider these five areas:

1. The Critic's identity
2. What the Critic sees as your problems in writing
3. What tricks the Critic uses to persuade you
4. How to get the Critic to go away
5. Any positive messages—compliments, gifts, etc.

This last area of questioning often brings forth unexpected responses.

Have a basic list of questions jotted down, but be prepared, as any good interviewer knows, to put them aside if you find the conversation taking you elsewhere. Let your questions flow fluently from the replies.

Keep your distance, especially in early interviews, by referring to yourself in the third person.

"What is it that you don't like about Kevin's writing?"
"How could Dorothy get rid of you?"
"What tricks do you use to get Allen to procrastinate?"

The Wall

Once again, as in all the major exercises of this book, watch out for the wall. Sure enough, right before the good stuff, the deep insight, the handle, the summit, your mind will try to trick you into thinking that there is nothing more there. When you (think you have) run out of things to say, questions to ask, Excelsior! That dry sensation is your tip that the best is yet to come. Excelsior! Ask your Critic outright, "Well, I have nothing more to ask you. Are you hiding something from me behind the wall?"

Closing—Three Steps

This first interview needs to be a minimum of twenty minutes. When your signal says that time is up, do three quick things before ending. First, thank your Critic for coming out of hiding and being willing to talk with you. It is only right that you acknowledge that, especially since you want to leave the lines of communication open for return visits.

Second, reunite with your Critic in some informal way. I do not want you to come out of this exercise feeling schizophrenic, and of course, the Critic is you. Prospero knew this in *The Tempest*. At the end of the play he decides to keep Caliban on the island with him: "This thing of darkness, I acknowledge mine." At the end of your twenty-minute interaction, reunite in simple fashion, saying, "We are one" or "Let's get back together now."

Third, make an appointment to meet again; set an actual, specific date and time. Maybe for breakfast the next morning, that evening before bed, at lunch on Wednesday. Actually enter that appointment later in your datebook; it is, as Dorothea Brande says of any appointment to write, "a debt of honor to be scrupulously discharged."

More than in any other exercise in this book so far, you need to suspend judgment about the outcome or procedure of this one. There is no "right" way to do this and no "wrong" way. Whatever happens is what is right for you. Maintain a playful pose, detached yet curious, like trying a new ethnic restaurant that smells intriguing when you pass it. No risk, no way to be wrong, and the good chance that something satisfying will reward your willingness to try.

Now, set the timer for twenty minutes, have a few set questions in mind, and then rapidwrite your way through the entire interview.

▶ **Progress Log:** Record your experience with your Critic. Note the time and date you scheduled to meet again.

EXAMPLES OF INTERVIEWS: PITFALLS AND PULLTHROUGHS

All the writing done during my workshop is private. Sometimes people are kind enough and generous enough to share their work with me. I am touched whenever anyone does that because I recognize the vulnerability involved, the laying bare of self.

The people quoted below have given me permission to share their interviews with their Critics in the hope that these excerpts would help you deal with yours. The individuals represented here come from different backgrounds and ambitions, yet their interviews have a remarkable commonality. None of them has ever seen the others' interviews, but the same motifs appear.

Victory is a therapist who secretly wants to write a novel; Richard, an archivist and Ph.D. candidate who, after taking my class, also became a songwriter; George, an attorney who applied his discoveries in handling the Critic directly to his courtroom interactions. Clarice was a bureaucrat who, after taking my course, realized a lifelong dream: she quit her job and now supports herself full-time with her freelance writing.

First, the Last Word

Never let the Critic have the last word. You are the one in control. When Victory did her interview in class, she forgot this principle and came up to me sadly after the exercise. "Now what do I do?" she moaned, handing me this.

Victory: What do you look like?

Critic: A whole group of family—grandmothers, uncles, brothers, stepmother.

Victory: What do you have to say to me?

Critic: That your writing is in bad taste. You shouldn't have to stoop to being coarse—if you had any talent, you could write the kind of work that would not offend anyone. This use of vulgar language and blatant sexuality shows a lack of skill and a baseness of personality. It's not that we're prudish; it's that your lifestyle, personality, and morals are questionable at best. I know you think you see and live life to the fullest, but we think you are an embarrassment.

That is no note to end an interview on!

"How come they got the last word?" I asked. "Go back to the interview again and give a rebuttal. Come back with an answer, any answer, but do not let the Critic have the last word."

So she went back to the interview and continued on with it. This time she took the reins firmly in hand and came back with a decisive retort.

Victory: That is nasty. I think you're jealous. I've made, am making, and will make horrendous mistakes—but at least I'm living—at least I'm alive. I don't care how trite that sounds—it's true. You are so provincial, so judgmental. I don't know how anyone can take you seriously. Unfortunately, I do. I do take you seriously. See, I care about you. I care about your opinion. You're nice people. It's just that you live a lifestyle that I could never be satisfied with. Not that mine is better—I wish all this stupid judging would cease. I can't live the life you approve of—a husband with the right job, cute kids who take swim lessons—saying and doing all the Junior League things.

I've chosen my path, and it's part of who I am. And who I am is a damn caring, loving, sensitive, funny, thinking woman. And I have things to say. Now, if you keep giving me all this crap, trying to make me feel guilty, just because you're not comfortable with what you hear, then we all lose. I get shut up and feel like a failure and you lose hearing an intelligent, articulate voice. So give me an f——ing chance.

Her chorus of Critics relented.

Stand up for yourself; believe in yourself. Do not be bullied by the Critic's sarcasm. Do not believe him when he lies to you. Call him on his lies and inform him squarely that you will not tolerate a relationship based on deceit.

Clarice: I don't want to seem harsh here, but you just lied to me. You said I've never published anything. I have. It may not be much, but I published a book review in a student journal, and I published several poems in high school.

Critic: Oh ho! So you caught me at it. All right, so I lied. I seem to get away with it most of the time. Absolutes are so easy to sell.

Clarice: Well, I would like you to consider carefully that I do not deserve to be lied to. If you are going to help me out, which I insist you do, I can't let you lie to me. Please take the attitude that I don't want absolutes and I don't want lies. I want you to give me honest evaluations of my progress. Absolutes don't help.

The Critic is humbled in the face of such strength, and Clarice establishes an excellent rapport with her Critic early on in the interview—a nice give-and-take is evident. Notice that the Critic does not let Clarice get away with anything either.

Clarice: I note a bit of amusement in your voice; you don't take me seriously. I want you to take me seriously.

Critic: Okay. As soon as you take yourself seriously.

And again, when Clarice sets a goal of writing every morning upon rising for at least fifteen minutes, the Critic calls her on that.

Critic: If you are serious about being a writer, fifteen minutes a day doesn't hack it.

Then he helps her, with more gentle nudging, to set her sights higher.

False Concessions

One recurring motif crops up so often in interviews with the Critic that I need to warn you to be on guard for it. I have seen this decoy any number of times in interviews with my own Critic and in virtually every interview that people have shared with me. It is the "I'll-be-good-if-you'll-be-great" bargain, and it is a wolf in the clothing of a lamb.

It goes like this: the Critic grudgingly makes a concession, supposedly giving you space and support, but there are strings attached. The agreement of support is a hollow promise, demanding unreasonable expectations on your part to fulfill. It is no bargain, believe me! It is a used-car-salesman pitch, and you need to defend yourself and not accept the terms. You have earned the reward without the conditions.

It is amazing how many Critics grudgingly agree to be supportive, provided the writer wins a Pulitzer Prize.

Critic: Maybe we could lighten up on you if you wrote like that guy, James Herriot, who wrote all those touching books.

Victory: I'd be proud to write like him, but that's just not me. That's not how I think—it would be forced and phoney. It could never be my best work. I wish you'd just face up to it. Accept it. Even give me a little support. I'm a pretty good writer, and if you'd lighten up on me, I could be an excellent writer. What do you say?

Critic: It's a lot to ask. Maybe. But for us to buy that, you'd better be really good—not mediocre. That maybe we could swallow. Maybe if you wrote something that won a Pulitzer Prize or something like that.

Richard's Critic was just as unrelenting.

Critic: I must be perfect and keep Richard perfect so he won't be open to criticism. I wouldn't mind his writing if he would just write perfectly, beautifully, wisely, profoundly. After all, anyone can write, but Richard has to be great, like Mark Twain, or Marcus Aurelius, or Hemingway, Borges, Steinbeck, all the so-called greats of literature—Shakespeare—you name it. They were smart and perfect. If Richard would write like that, I would ease up my criticism of him.

You need support free and clear, and you deserve nothing less. Respond to the Critic's phoney bargain. Answer back! Cut the strings! Do not accept those conditional terms.

Victory: Do you realize the pressure that puts on me? That is just a tad unrealistic, don't you think? *Maybe* I will write something that outstanding, but I've got to have the leeway to write all *kinds* of things—some of them maybe not even up to mediocre. That's how I'll get better, that's how I'll learn. I'm sick of this whole conversation; all you do is throw up more obstacles in my path—I don't know what you think you're accomplishing.

Critic: Okay, okay, we'll give you a chance. Just promise you'll really try hard. No half-hearted shot. Give it everything you've got. We're talking hard work here. Do you think you can work a little self-discipline into this fascinating life of yours?

Victory: Okay. You're right on this. I will really do my best. Believe it. And keep believing it. Thanks for the words. See you again on Sunday.

Richard exchanged the hollow bargain for a gift, detailed below.

False Friend

To my mind, one of the most insidious and despicable poses of the Critic is the "I-only-want-to-be-your-friend" disguise. This is often a difficult charge to respond to, because it is true that you need the Critic, but on decidedly different terms. If listening to his advice is keeping you from writing, he is no friend. Listen to George's Critic:

Critic: But you know that you need me. If it weren't for me, how would you keep from making a fool of yourself? How would you be sure to do a good job? If you just let yourself write whatever you wanted to write, how would you keep it from being gibberish? If you don't need to do things well in order to be liked by other people, how do you expect to continue to do things well?

Richard's Critic sings the same song.

Richard: Don't you think that Richard is old enough and smart enough to handle his own situation, problems, life, and writing, without your interference?

Critic: Well, he may be old enough, but he still needs me. He needs me to protect him from others and his own lack of sight. I am his excuse for not performing and succeeding.

This form of hit-and-run driving often takes your breath away. Do not lie in the street shaking your fist. Get up and run after the culprit. For example, this was George's answer when Ollie, his Critic, tried that line:

George: I think you're scared, Ollie. Of course, I am, too. You are finding my doubts—you should be able to because you've been with me an awful long time. You're scared because you're afraid that I won't need you now that I've learned your game and therefore you won't continue to exist. You're fighting for your life. Don't worry. While I may know your name and your game, I'm sure you'll continue to show up. And I know I will continue to perform well, not because of you, but because I want to. I know the pleasure that can come from doing anything well. I like that feeling and I want to experience it. I want to be thought of by myself and others as a success, not because success is important or because people like you if you are successful, but because it's fun to be successful.

Hit-and-Run Driving

The Critic likes to smash you and walk away, leaving you wounded. Set new standards: no hit-and-run driving allowed! Do not limp silently away. Acknowledge the blows that you can learn from; deflect back the others.

Critic: You are too afraid of failure to really be sucessful. You can be a small-time wonder. You can do those things that are easy and foreseeable for you, but you're too afraid to fall on your face, particularly with everyone watching, to really go for the big time.

George: Good one, Ollie. I have to give you credit. You certainly hit me there. I know I've stopped dreaming of the things I could do or be and have only looked at what I know that I can accomplish. I'm going to change that—but in a realistic manner. First, I have to deal with you.

And I hate to see you stoop to this, but name-calling works both ways.

Critic: Great Philosopher, enlighten me on the road to happiness. You get yourself caught up in ideas of happiness—of how you are going to write great things, do great things, and then you are "happy." The problem is that you never get those things written, never get those things done. No self-discipline. You're not willing to make the sacrifices necessary to get the job done. Great concepts, no performance. Or, more accurately, great concepts, good start, *no finish.* You would be a great "rabbit" in a record-breaking mile run.

George: You certainly are sharp today, fatso. Of course, you are right. But not completely. After all, Samuel Johnson continually berated himself for his laziness and sloth. He felt he was accomplishing nothing. Based on an absolute measurement, my life is pretty worthless— but almost everyone's is. But just because I can't perform up to my ideal standard does not mean I don't have to perform at all. I'm going to fail, have false starts, sit when I should be doing. But that's not going to excuse me from getting up and starting again. And I'm going to finish some of the things I start. Others I won't; they can wait.

Critic: Oh, you pompous fool. Just let reality intrude on your dreamworld and watch it collapse. In any case, your first big test is this proposal you are writing right now. Are you going to make the time and find the ability to sell your plan? I doubt it.

George: Watch my smoke! Time's up, fatso. See you on Wednesday morning. Thanks for the motivation.

The Half-Empty Glass

To the Critic the proverbial glass filled to the midline is always halfempty rather than half-full. It is up to you to catch him at this game and insist that some regard be given to positive steps you have taken.

This is what I call the Fabric Book Syndrome: the insistence on nothing but excellence is why the beautiful fabric-covered blank book you got for Christmas is still empty by June. Nothing-but-excellence does not motivate excellence; it motivates nothing.

Clarice: Hello, Critic. I'm back. I've got a few more of Henriette's questions to ask you. Is it all right to start in?

Critic: Certainly. Go right ahead.

Clarice: How do you make me believe you when I let you give me negative messages?

Critic: I point to all the negative evidence—the pure fact that you've never published anything—and then make it seem as if there is an endless gulf between where you are (i.e., "unpublished") and where you want to be (i.e., "winner of the Nobel Prize for literature"). Until you find a thread to tie the two together you will continue to stay on one side of the gulf.

Clarice soon tires of the Critic's negativity and finally comes right out and asks him for some positive feedback.

Clarice: It's time for a few more questions, but first I would like you to assess my first week's efforts in positive terms. Don't tell me what I didn't do; tell me what I did and did right.

Critic: All right. You got up early and wrote for fifteen minutes each morning of the work week without regard to the quality of the writing. In addition, you put in fifteen minutes on Saturday even though it was not promised. You also resumed our conversations for the most part as promised.

If you worry too much about being perfect, perhaps these two stories will free you to lighten up and make a few mistakes. I am told that an exquisite Turkish tapestry hangs at the United Nations. Only the tour guide can find the deliberate mistake in the lower corner. "To make the tapestry perfect would be an affront to Allah," he explains. In the same vein, Irish knitters, when crafting a sweater, also deliberately incorporate a mistake, for "only God is perfect." So tell your Critic you do not want your work to be sacrilegious; a mistake or two helps keep you humble.

Rewards

Ask for clarification, keep on the track, do not accept pushiness. Be assertive. It pays to persevere at the interview with the Critic. For one thing, the techniques you use to deal with his often-abrasive personality are extremely useful in coping with difficult people in general, so it is good training for you to learn how not to let yourself get trampled. As people improve their relationships with their Critics, I suspect they may generally improve their own self-esteem and make parallel changes in their interactions with combative people in their lives.

Also, since the Critic works in other areas of your life besides writing, the freedom you achieve when you silence him here will definitely extend to the goals and dreams you have in other areas. An office manager at a large hospital wrote to me after a workshop:

> Oh, yes, I am becoming acquainted with my Critic. It is a leprechaun, male, wearing a green suit, a black hat, and Robin Hood shoes. His name is Perversity. Perversity and I have some straightening out to do. He has been very active in my life. Not only in writing but in other areas *where he does not need to be*.

Transformation

Finally—and I can document this from personal experience, as well as from hundreds of interviews people have shared with me—as you change your relationship with your Critic, the Critic changes in his interactions with you. Over the years, the Critic actually becomes less combative, more supportive. One writer I know shared with me some early interviews in which the Critic was punching her in the stomach. After five years of interviews, you would hardly recognize this couple now. Her Critic affirms her, agrees that she is progressing nicely, exclaims over her good passages, says "Kudos to you!" at her smallest victory. Of course, he still goads her on and keeps her mindful of her goals, but their relationship is truly adult to adult.

The four interviewers quoted above all report their relationships with their Critic have improved. Clarice, for example, now goes to her Critic every morning, to help her set the day's goals and establish a reasonable work schedule. He is on her side. Richard was astonished when he asked his Critic for a gift and received the most extraordinary present, which he cherishes to this day.

Gentle yet firm insistence that you will not let the Critic get the upper hand leads gracefully to such magnificent conversations as this:

Richard: If you were to give the writer Richard a gift, what would you give him?

Critic: Well, I think he would like me to give him a Ph.D. But that's the laziness in him. I say I'd like to give him courage, courage to write freely. For one thing, that will take him through a Ph.D. and beyond, throughout his writing life.

The Critic says that Richard must earn this gift, but Richard persuades him to give it to him now; the gift itself will help him be worthy of it. So the Critic concedes:

Critic: He must have the courage to write, courage to work hard at the job of writing, when he's tired, bored; courage to learn new words and to use old ones better; courage to read other writers and learn from them, not be intimidated by them; courage to face the Critic;

courage to face himself; courage to write things that anyone, everyone—or *no one*—may read. He must have courage to be called a fool by any and all; courage always to write his best; courage to write freely and without inhibition; courage to be financially successful at his writing. He must have courage for all that—and more. I have the power to grant it. I have that amount to spare, and much more. I have infinite courage to write. So I lose nothing by granting a good amount to the writer Richard.

I do so here grant it, now, in this pen, in these words, on this paper. He may here read my grant if he ever questions his memory of it. What is granted will not be taken away.

Richard: Thank you, Mr. Critic. I call you Mister out of respect. You shall be honored by your gift. I shall use it freely and wisely. I thank you most sincerely from the bottom of my heart and from the top of my mind. My self is no less divided, but is more harmonious for the gift.

But let's not be too gullible here; Richard was smart enough to have this grant notorized, in triplicate, and it serves him well to this day. You are welcome to ask your Critic for a similar boon. Be brave! You deserve it.

CHAPTER 8

Re-Vision: Caliban Returns, at Your Invitation

There are days when the result is so bad that no fewer than five revisions are required. In contrast, when I'm greatly inspired, only four revisions are needed.

—JOHN KENNETH GALBRAITH

Let's get one thing straight from the start: it's okay to need editing. What you wrote in rapidwriting, using rumination, after talking back to the Critic, is very likely only a draft—and *that's okay*. What you wrote was written with the understanding that it need not be perfect, and that, in fact, is what gave it its flow. The judgment that you *ought* to be able to write perfectly and well right out the door is what impedes flow—the flow of words in terms of abundance and in terms of style.

So lighten up on yourself when it comes to the editing part. If you need a lot of revision, congratulate yourself on being so prolific. Congratulate yourself on your spontaneity, your profusion. And then roll up your sleeves and get to work.

A MATTER OF ATTITUDE

Editing invites the left side of your brain—the logical side—to return with you to your written piece and offer specific advice on improvement and rearrangement. Remember, though, Caliban returns now at your invitation, as your guest, and so he comes back as your friend. The difference between this sort of editing and the premature edit voice is that, where before the edit voice put you down, now Caliban is ready to offer adult-to-adult suggestions on improving your writing.

This book's editor exemplified in the most powerful and life-giving way the kind of critic we can be to ourselves in our own editing when we go at it with mutual respect. In our correspondence, my editor called himself "the nagging voice of the Critic"—but he was never that. He was never the mean and dispiriting voice of the Critic of chapter 7. When he returned my manuscript with his suggested corrections, this was the opening paragraph of the cover letter:

Congratulations on writing a beautiful, breathtaking book. I don't know if I will ever see the writing process the same again after reading it. It undulates throughout with your voice, your enthusiasm, your excitement, your friendliness. It is "supportive" in the best sense, never demeaning or discouraging: it sends me out there thinking I can write anything, even this letter to its author. . .

. . . telling me everything I needed to correct, amend, revise, restore, elaborate, eliminate, clarify, and support. I was ready; I was primed for it. Wouldn't you be?

Take that opening paragraph. Wrap it around you. Feel snug and warm inside of it. And now tell me. Would you be willing to make the corrections suggested by such an editor?

In fact, the words "never demeaning or discouraging" apply equally to my editor's contribution. And to that I could add, "never demanding," for he continually couched his comments in such qualifiers as "I think you need. . . "; "Maybe you could note. . . "; "Would you be willing to . . . " He raised important questions without supplying answers; he trusted me to provide the answers. "This is confusing here." "Could you clarify?" "Something's missing. Please supply the transition." "Can you construct some link between this chapter and the previous one? Do you think a link is necessary? I guess I thought the transition was a bit bumpy, and I like it when chapters hook up. If none seems natural, forget it." He always left me with the good feeling that I was the one in charge; the options of choice were mine.

What I am asking you to do is to be that same kind of gentle, practical friend to yourself when you edit your own writing. Kenneth Koch, who teaches children in New York City to write poetry, has this lovely line: when helping students edit, he has them read their own work aloud and then asks, "How can I help you?"

Even a young writer often knows herself the trouble spots in her piece, what is working and what is not working; it changes the temper of the conference from the outset for the teacher to come at the editing task with such a tone. Now the student need not defend to the death the opening paragraph that, deep in her heart, she is not pleased with, either.

How can I help you?

Are you willing to ask yourself that same patient and respectful question and trust that the answer is wise?

It is in that light, and with that attitude, that this chapter reviews the whole-brained writing process and presents some tips and techniques that will be helpful at the editing point in your venture.

WHOLE-BRAINED WRITING: THE FIVE R'S

Every piece that you write, whether it is a short memo or a long treatise, a letter to your grandmother or a legal brief, will benefit from following the Five R's of whole-brained writing. Whole-brained writing follows an alternating pattern, using the strengths of the right, then the left, then the right, then the left again. The process is like a measured march. Left-right-left-right-left-right-left: a marching cadence of the brain.

Many of you already follow this pattern naturally without being aware of it. What I want to do is bring the process into awareness, so that you may consciously follow the steps that will put you back in command of your writing.

Follow these five steps religiously for a dramatic increase in fluency and persuasion.

1. Ruminate
2. Rapidwrite
3. Retreat
4. Revise
5. Repeat

1. RUMINATE, THEN 2. RAPIDWRITE

Steps 1 and 2 put into practice much of what you have learned so far in this book. By now I trust you realize that the rumination stage, sometimes called prewriting, is integral to the writing task and needs to be acknowledged as part of the process. This is the time for staring out the window, taking a shower, thinking about your ideas in a most general way, and also thinking about your audience. In a low-key, desultory fashion, address such questions as

What are some of the things I want this writing to accomplish?
What are some of the points I want to cover?
What effect will it have on my readers?

The word *rumination* comes from the Latin word *rumen*, which is the cow's second stomach. Be like the contented bovine, chewing meditatively on her cud, gazing serenely into the distance, *sans souci*, without concern.

Follow this musing with rapidwriting. "Power it out" past the Critic, get words on paper. Jot your ideas down even if they seem disorganized; put down your doubts and hesitancy right along with the initial text. Do your branching, too, in the same brainstorming fashion as the nonstop writing. This is not a time for judgment or evaluation: put the editing side of your brain on hold.

3. RETREAT: THE SECOND "SILENT TIME"

Retreat by stepping back or away from your manuscript. To do so is not to desert, but to regroup. This extraordinarily important step in the writing process is too often underplayed or omitted altogether. Retreat is imperative to the quality and the effectiveness of the finished product, and it is the one step that hurried executives and other busy writers think they can dispense with. Wrong! This third step in the cycle of composition gives you new perspective and makes revision (rē-vision) live up to its name. Rē-vision: to look at again. Take a step back or away from your manuscript, turn your attention to other matters, and come back renewed, to look at it again. Come back fresh, ready to judge the impact of your words exactly as the intended audience will.

Once I saw a cartoon that depicted a businessman with his feet up on the desk and his hands behind his head. The caption read, "I may not look busy, but I've got eighteen people on hold right now." When you retreat, you let your writing age: "I may not look busy, but I have a manuscript on hold right now."

I tell the people I work with that this period of retreat from the manuscript, of moving away and letting your paper "age," is *nonnegotiable*— it is that important and that imperative. The retreat that I refer to is more a psychological apartness than a period of time away; turn your attention, even momentarily, to something else. Ideally, if your schedule permits, let your words lie fallow overnight (Dorothea Brande suggests a week!), but even if you do not have that luxury of time, do not eliminate this step. Get up from your work table, walk away a moment, take a deep breath, and return. Shift your attention away from what you have written, and when you return to it, whether it is the next day or only several moments later, you will see it with a new eye.

It is an ingredient of genius to recognize the importance of retreat. You are in good company when you include this element in your work style. Julian Jaynes recounts stories about Helmholtz and Einstein and the great mathematicians Gauss and Poincaré, all of whom experienced remarkable breakthroughs in their work after putting it aside for a while and not thinking about it at all. The project was worked on, then forgotten, before the final illumination that brought it to fruition. "Indeed," says Jaynes, "it is sometimes almost as if the problem had to be forgotten to be solved."

Charles Brooks says that writing is a kind of "back-stove cookery." He continues his *pot au feu* metaphor by describing how our words simmer over a little flame:

Pieces of this and that, an odd carrot, as it were, a leftover potato, a pithy bone, discarded trifles, are tossed in from time to time to feed the composition. Raw paragraphs, when they have stewed all night, at last become tender to the fork.[1]

And, as a wit in one of my workshops added, "Then you can skim the fat off the top!"

4. REVISE

Now that you have let your piece simmer, return to it refreshed; "re-vision" it, look at it again.

I want you to come back at this point in a different frame of mind, *as though you were reading this document for the first time,* as though you were its primary audience, not its author.

As you read your work for the first time, how does it hit you? Is the meaning clear? Does it move you to act, or to feel at one with the writer? Does the rhythm fall nicely on your ear? Is there a buildup, a crescendo, and a sense of completion at the end?

Do not make corrections now; simply mark the "pings"—the places where sense or sentence goes awry, where meaning is obscured, where the tone somehow offends. Sometimes you can actually feel a physical ping in your stomach at the parts that do not fit; other times it is a little bell in your head. Simply put a check mark in the margin wherever that unsettling sensation occurs. Notice that you are not making any judgments here about the author's means of expression; you are only quietly noting the areas that are weak or confusing. Using some of the editing pointers detailed below, you will then be able to go back and strengthen those weak spots, correct the tone, and get your message across with power.

5. REPEAT

Repeat these steps as often as time allows and the importance of your piece dictates. For most business letters, memos, and the like, once is usually sufficient. For longer communications, more weighty matters, you might want to go through these steps several times, each time honing further your editing skills and listening ear. If you have limited time available, divide it accordingly, but do not eliminate a step to compensate. Whatever your time frame, adapting all five steps to fit it assures that your words will have impact and be worth reading.

IN MEDIAS RES: VIEWS OF A WORK IN PROGRESS

In his book *Writing Well,* William Zinsser generously presents some typed pages from his manuscript in the stages of editing. Just seeing those pages was so heartening to me that, in the same spirit, I want to share some versions of my work so you will know that it did not arrive on the page as a finished product. The edited versions appear on pages 94 to 95. The final product is on pages 93 and 96.

EDITING TIPS AND TECHNIQUES

The goal of all writing, according to Horace, is to be *"dulce et utile"*—palatable as well as useful. Chaucer promised as much when his host, Harry Bailey, offered a prize of free supper to the Canterbury pilgrim who could tell the tale of "best sentence and moost solaas": the best instruction and highest amusement. It is not classical and medieval writers alone who know the import of this standard. For over thirty years, *Highlights for Children* has published this banner on each and every cover: "Fun with a Purpose."

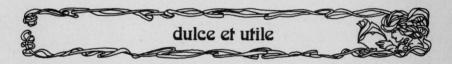

dulce et utile

When you edit, keep this norm in mind. The bottom line of all writing, whether you are selling information or ideas, is the answer to this question: does it persuade pleasantly, does it educate and entertain?

You make your piece *"dulce"* by capturing a rhythm. Listen to how you words fall on the ear. Recite your piece out loud, or have someone read it to you. Entertain with metaphors, rhetorical "colors"; use expressions appropriate to your audience so that the reader has the distinct sense of one human being addressing another human being. No matter how technical your subject matter, this last ingredient is absolutely essential to effective writing. Somehow your words need to convey that you care for and respect not only the subject but the reader as well. The editing tips and professional tricks of the trade outlined in this chapter will help do this almost by osmosis.

You make your piece *"utile"* if you respect clarity and are ruthless about clutter. Your writing educates, persuades, and has a purpose when you care impeccably about your logic and the progression of your thoughts. In this regard, the section on fallacies will aid you; "Strip Mining" will show you how to put your ideas in order.

IMPROVE YOUR WRITING INSTANTLY IN THREE EASY LESSONS

I can recommend several books on clear and effective writing, most notably William Zinsser's *On Writing Well* and Strunk and White's *Elements of Style*. A fine, slender guide to good business writing is Ellen Roddick's *Writing That Means Business: A Manager's Guide*. Some of the best pure grammar books were written in the 1940s and 1950s. As in

VERSION 1

~~Instant~~ Improvement *Your Writing Instantly* (START)

~~I could sum up the general malaise of business writing~~ clean up
~~considerably with three basic rules.~~ There are entire books written on
clear *& effective* writing, most notably *Wm.* Zinsser; *On Writ Well* and Strunk and White.'s *Elem / Style* I would also
recommend as a general guide Ellen Roddick's *incl index* or a good old-fashioned
grammar book from a used bookstore for ~~those finer points that plague you~~ *like etiquette books - don't change - picayune*
Keep one or several ~~of these books as a reference~~ on you desk. ~~They will~~
~~help you fine-tune your piece or answer questions about usage.~~

~~In the corporate, legal and hospital world, the writing that I see in~~
~~my work, there are 3 major malaise areas where dramatic improvement is~~
~~realized.~~ Putting all the writing books aside for a moment, I want to
pintpoint three major areas of malaise where corporate prose (bogs) down, and
if you never did another thing to your business writing but ~~bring~~ these *change in*
three ~~into your awareness~~ *areas*, I guarantee a major improvement in the
effectiveness of your ~~prose~~ *writing.* ~~If you are like the majority of corporate~~
~~writers, this is where your writing bogs down.~~ Each time I give a~~n~~ *in-house*
workshop, the company I am working for submits to me ~~three~~ *several* weeks ahead
samples of their writing, and I put together a handbook for that firm based
on their own writing strengths and weaknesses. ~~I am never at a loss for~~
~~examples of these three areas~~ I have yet to work with the company that
did not unwittingly furnish a good supply of these atrotricities of prose.
I am never at a loss for examples. ~~Often one paragraph from the top~~
~~manager supplies me with all three~~ ~~(how not to write~~ ~~samples.)~~ *examples* Often I am
able to glean from a single paragraph from the top manager all three. this
stinks says caliban no flow. Oh well, maybe I at least learned one way not
to invent an electric light bulb. And there are only 999 attempts left.

VERSION 2

Improve Your Writing Instantly *in 3 Easy Lessons*

There are entire books written on clear and effective writing, most
notably William Zinsser's <u>On Writing Well</u> and Strunk and White's <u>Elements</u>
<u>of Style.</u> Some of the best pure grammar books were written in the 1940's
and 1950's. ~~Like~~ *As in* a good book of etiquette, the examples and specific
applications may change, but the rules hold sound, and the underlying
principles do not change with the fashion. I suggest that if you are
looking for a solid, readable grammar ~~reference book, you~~ get an old, used
one from a used bookstore. Keep it on your desk for those picayune points
that plague you.

Not nearly as comprehensive as those ancient tomes, but a fine,

slender guide to good writing ~~published by Macmillan~~ is Ellen Roddick's
Writing that Means Business: A Manager's Guide. Ms. Roddick gives hints to
make your business writing more forceful and clear; the book includes a
useful index.

    Putting all the writing books aside for a moment, I want to pinpoint
three major ~~areas of malaise~~ *places* where corporate prose bogs down, and if you
never did another thing to your business writing but ~~change~~ *make* ~~in these three~~ *there*
~~areas,~~ I guarantee ~~a major improvement in the effectiveness of~~ *that* your
writing. *will be more effective* Each time I give an in-house workshop, ~~the company~~ ~~I am working~~
~~for submits to me several weeks ahead samples of their writing, and~~ I put
together a handbook for that firm based on their own writing strengths and
weaknesses. ~~I have yet to work with the company that did not unwittingly~~
~~furnish a good supply of these atrocities of prose.~~ I am never at a loss
for examples *of atrocious prose.* Often I am able to glean from a single paragraph from the
top manager all three how not to write examples.

VERSION 3

Improve Your Writing Instantly in Three Easy Lessons

passive voice! ~~There are entire~~ *I can recommend several* books ~~written~~ on clear and effective writing, most
notably William Zinsser's On Writing Well and Strunk and White's Elements
of Style. ~~Not nearly as comprehensive as those ~ncient tomes, but~~ A fine,
slender guide to good *business* writing is Ellen Roddick's Writing That Means
Business: A Manager's Guide. ~~Ms. Roddick gives hints to make your business~~
~~writing more forceful and clear; the book includes a useful index.~~ Some of
the best pure grammar books were written in the 1940's and 1950's. As in a
good book of etiquette, the examples and ~~specific~~ applications may change,
but the rules hold sound, and the underlying principles do not change with
the fashion. I suggest that if you are looking for a solid, readable
grammar, get an old ~~used~~ one from a used bookstore. Keep it on your desk
for those picayune points that plague you.

    Putting all the writing books aside for a moment, I want to pinpoint
three major places where corporate prose bogs down, and if you never did
another thing to your ~~business~~ writing but make changes there, I guarantee
that your writing will be more effective. Each time I give an in-house
workshop, I put together a handbook *of the* for that firm ~~based on their own~~
~~based on samples furnished in advance~~ *to illustrate*
writing strengths and weaknesses. I am never at a loss for examples ~~of~~
these 3 areas. ~~atrocious prose.~~ Often I am able to glean from a single paragraph from the
top manager all three ~~how not to write~~ examples *of how not to write.*

a good book of etiquette, the examples and applications may change, but the rules hold sound, and the underlying principles do not change with the fashion. I suggest that if you are looking for a solid, readable grammar, get an old one from a used bookstore. Keep it on your desk for those picayune points that plague you.

Putting all the writing books aside for a moment, I want to pinpoint three places where corporate prose bogs down, and if you never do another thing to your writing but make changes there, I guarantee that your writing will be more effective. Each time I give an in-house workshop, I put together a handbook of the firm's writing strengths and weaknesses, based on samples furnished in advance. I am never at a loss for examples to illustrate these three areas. I am often able to glean, from a single paragraph by the top manager, all three examples of how not to write.

The members of every law firm, corporation, hospital, and school administration I work with make dramatic differences in their communication by incorporating these three rules. If you want your writing to be clear, concise, and persuasive;

1. Avoid the passive voice
2. Trim the fat
3. Watch parallels

1. Avoid the Passive Voice

Notice how many guides for business writing today (see articles in *Byte, U.S. News and World Report,* and *Business Week* magazines and the book *Be Twice as Smart as You Are* as examples) instruct the writer to "be conversational." One thing they mean by that is avoid the passive voice, for the active voice is the voice of one person speaking to another.

In active voice sentences, the subject comes first, so you know up front who is doing the action of the verb ("I have noticed. . . "; "The managers of X Department report that. . . "). The passive voice hides the subject; the reader has an uneasy sense that there are no people around ("It has come to my attention. . . "; "It has been reported. . . ").

The passive voice is convoluted; it takes the energy out of your writing and makes your message flaccid. It is absolutely homicidal—it kills the people in your prose. What you are left with is two robots communicating; "An effort has been made, machine, to bring to your attention. . . " "Please be advised, machine, that your bill is overdue." The passive voice invariably comes across as pontificating, patronizing, talking down. It sounds insincere, even dishonest, and it makes the reader uncomfortable, not trusting, though usually the reader cannot put her finger on why.

Active verbs are stronger, shorter, more direct, and more personal.

They convey conviction and acknowledge responsibility, engendering confidence and security in your reader.

Of course, the passive voice is sometimes necessary and useful. There are times, especially in legal documents, when you do not want to assume responsibility for anything. My favorite example of this came from a property management letter:

Of added benefit was that a turnover was created by the increase, bringing a higher quality tenant.

You have to admit that is a clever, nonlitigious way to say

We raised the rent and threw the deadbeats out.

Perhaps a more chilling example of avoiding responsibility was the now-famous stark four-sentence report from the Council of Ministers in Moscow after the accident at Chernobyl. Several days after the incident, this terse statement "was issued":

An accident *has taken* place at the Chernobyl power station, and one of the reactors *was damaged*. Measures *are being taken* to eliminate the consequences of the accident. Those affected by it *are being given* assistance. A government commission *has been set up*.[2]

If you need to use the passive voice, use it judiciously; it has a tendency to snowball. Open your letter with "Enclosed is. . . ," followed by a tangle of prepositional phrases, and the next six deadly sentences march right into passive place. Start instead with the active voice ("I enclose. . . ") and what follows will be more natural and "conversational."

2. Trim the Fat

Keep the report short and concise. The Gettysburg Address required only 266 words; the Ten Commandments, 297 words; the Declaration of Independence, 300 words, and the order of the U. S. Office of Price Administration to reduce the price of cabbage, 26,911 words.

—Unknown

Periphrasis obfuscates! (Two wonderful words that do what they tell you not to!) Challenge yourself, when you go back over a written piece, to eliminate or tighten as much as 50 percent of your words. Think of it as energizing rather than defeating. Are you equal to the challenge?

Peter Elbow avers that for every word you cut, one more reader stays with you. In my first editing round, I set a goal to cut at least seventy-five words from each page; I want seventy-five more readers per page to stay with me.

Here are some flags to watch for:

• *Too many prepositions* usually means there are not enough "working words" in a sentence: too much mortar and not enough bricks. This letter came home from school; I had to read it over several times before I knew what it said.

As a result *of* Public Law 875, entitlement *from* the Federal government contributes *to* our general fund budget and it behooves us to make every effort to receive our full entitlement *for* this district *for* this year. [5 prepositions]

Present reporting methods require that we gather the information indicated *on* the accompanying card *on* one date *in* October. We are particularly interested *in* cards *of* pupils whose parents worked *on* federal property *on* October 1st. Since certain phases *of* eligibility *in* other categories require interpretation, we ask that all cards be returned. [9 prepositions]

Attention is called *to* the fact that regulations permit eligibility *for* federal payment *in* the instance *of* a parent coming *to* our school district as a member *of* the armed forces and leaving *for* duty outside *of* this area while the family retains its residence *in* this district. [9 prepositions; *Total:* 23 prepositions, 138 words]

Why not this, instead?

Each year, the Federal Government (Public Law 875) contributes *to* our general fund budget. We need to contact every family to receive the district's full entitlement. [1 preposition]

Please fill out the enclosed card, even if you do not believe that you are eligible, especially if your parents worked *on* federal property *on* October 1st. [2 prepositions]

Even if one *of* the parents is *in* the military and does not live *with* the family, the district is still entitled *to* federal payment. [4 prepositions; *Total:* 7 prepositions, 78 words]

Instead of

Please excuse my delay *in* responding *to* your request *for* examples *of* the charting format used *at* General Hospital Emergency Department. [5 prepositions] Attached *for* your review are two examples *of* actual patient records. [2 prepositions; *Total:* 7 prepositions, 32 words]

Try

Please excuse my delayed response *to* your request *for* charting format examples. [2 prepositions] I have attached two examples *of* actual patient records used *at* General Hospital. [2 prepositions; *Total:* 4 prepositions, 25 words]

Instead of

This information sheet was prepared to introduce you *to* the nomenclature *of* patient problem identification which has been adopted *by* the Nursing Department *at* General Hospital. [*Total:* 4 prepositions; 26 words]

Try

The Nursing Department *at* General Hospital has adopted a system *of* identifying patient problems; this information sheet introduces you *to* that system. [*Total:* 3 prepositions; 22 words]

Lawyers are especially fond of multiple prepositions, which tend to confuse rather than clarify.

In the event that there is a waiver *of* the attorney-client privilege *by* the client, the letters must be produced *by* the attorney *for* the purpose *of* inspection *by* the adversary party. [*Total:* 7 prepositions; 33 words][3]

That could possibly be changed to

If the client waives the attorney-client privilege, the attorney must produce letters *for* the adversary party to inspect. [*Total:* 1 preposition; 19 words]

Often two prepositions close to each other stretch out the work of one: learn to spot these elongated expressions and substitute the singular (for example, "by means of" = "by"; "for the purpose of" = "for").

• Of course, *passive voice* is always wordier, because you need a helping verb (*was* prepared, *has been* adopted, *must be* produced) and often a prepositional string (by the Nursing Department, by the adversary party) to support it, so eliminating the passive voice kills two obfuscatory birds with one stone.

• *Qualifiers or empty intensifiers* are what E. B. White, in a classic phrase, labels "leeches that infest the pond of prose, sucking the blood of words."[4] Be on your guard against *very, quite,* and that bane of vitality, *really.* Notice how much more vigor your sentences have when you eliminate these bloodsuckers.

It was really a pleasure to meet with you. It is very unfortunate that we will not be able to put your plan into immediate operation. We were most pleased to have been able to assist you this far, and trust there will be other opportunities. As you are aware, we have relatively frequent contact with virtually all of our offices in other states, which might be of help to you.

Take out *really, very, most, relatively,* and *virtually,* and hear how much sharper it reads.

3. Watch Parallels

You throw your readers off balance when you neglect the relationship of words in your sentence or headings on your paper. Whenever you list or use headings and subheadings, apply the prepositions, articles, and verbs consistently. For example, this sentence is unsettling:

The overall objective of the audit was to determine the store's effectiveness in meeting customer needs, compliance with company policies, and providing adequate internal controls of daily store operations.

The single change of *compliance* to *complying* makes this list parallel and contributes immeasurably to its smoothness and sense.

It is totally embarassing when a description of a writing course is poorly written, but I had the word *including* before *developing* in the copy I gave to the editor of the college bulletin, and I suppose the copy editor, to economize, chose to omit it. This completely nonparallel course description, to my mortification, ran:

Dr. Klauser's class will address how to write and sell articles, developing saleable ideas, slanting, writing a query letter and dealing with editors.

Headings and subheadings in a paper, chapter, or memo also read better when you keep in mind the guideline of parallel construction (as in "*Avoid* the Passive Voice," "*Trim* the Fat," "*Watch* Parallels").

EXERCISE 12: IMPROVE THIS SAMPLE

Using the following sample, or one of your own, change the passive voice to the active, slash the number of prepositions, compact the wordiness and repetition, and correct the faulty parallelism:

In today's situation, there is still a lack of understanding by many of our employees and publics about the way this program is being managed. This is evidenced by polarized interests, increased appeals, litigation, violence, etc. There needs to be a major focus for our information and education program that helps people easily understand our mission; some of the laws and regulations under which we manage; the many successes in our management and some of the failures, and what corrective measures are being taken; a better understanding of our planning process; how public input is used; and in what ways our agency is providing for public interests.

TONE

Tone is a matter of respect for the reader. Sometimes writers are rude without realizing it. Read your letter or memo or whatever back to yourself out loud. Are you offended?

If you are conscious of your audience, and if you incorporate the three rules detailed above into your writing, the tone will take care of itself.

For example, a letter begun in passive voice already sets the tone for distancing and coolness. I knew an executive director who began every letter he wrote with this chilling phrase: "Reference is made to your. . . " With such an opener, the rest of the letter was sure to be arch and diffident.

If you need to say something harsh, often the simple expedient of putting the harsh word in the middle of the letter softens the blow.

THE FOG INDEX

The Fog Index is a useful tool for rating your writing and gauging the level of obscurity in your prose. Developed by Robert Gunning of

Columbus, Ohio, to guide newspaper writers, the Fog Index is an actual mathematical formula that you can apply to any writing sample to determine the *grade level* that it takes to easily understand what you just wrote.[5]

To use the Fog Index, pick a sample of writing about 100–125 words long. Count the number of words in succeeding sentences: for example, $8 + 21 + 11 + 3 + 19 + 7 + 23 + 10 = 102$ words in 8 sentences. Dates and other number combinations count as single words. Independent clauses qualify as separate sentences. "In school we studied; we learned; we improved" is three sentences. Divide the total words by the number of sentences: in the example, 102 words divided by 8 sentences equals 13 words, the average sentence length.

Next, count the number of words that have three or more syllables. Do not include words made up of short words, such as *yellowtail* or *pawnbroker*. Also, do not include polysyllabic words that begin a sentence; proper names; or verbs made into three syllables by adding *-es* or *-ed* (for example, *concluded*). Divide this count by the passage length to get the *percentage* of long words. For example, if you counted 16 polysyllables out of 102 words, you would divide 16 by 102 and get 15 percent.

Now add the average sentence length to the percentage of long words. Multiply the total by 0.4 to get the grade level of reading comprehension. (Ignore the digits following the decimal point; do not round off numbers.) In our example, $13 + 15 = 28$; $28 \times 0.4 = 11$.

The Fog Index is relative. There is no right or wrong score, although I personally get a little tight around the collar with any score over 15. If you are writing to an educated, but not an erudite audience, 11 or 12 is an appropriate level. *Harper's* and *Atlantic Monthly* are 12; *Time, Business Week,* and the *Wall Street Journal* average 11. For a general audience, 10 seems about right: the Gettysburg Address and Reader's Digest both have a Fog Index of 10. Most best-selling books have a Fog Index of from 8 to 10.

> 1. Choose a sample 100–125 words long.
> 2. Count the words and sentences. Count the independent clauses as separate sentences. Divide the word count by the sentence count.
> 3. Count words of three or more syllables. Divide by the length of the passage to get the percentage. Add this to the average sentence length.
> 4. Multiply the total by 0.4.
>
> (Product: The grade level needed for easy comprehension, or the Fog Index.)

EXERCISE 13: APPLY THE FOG INDEX TO YOUR OWN WRITING

Using the chart, apply the Fog Index to a paragraph or two of your own writing. Is your score higher or lower than you anticipated? Pick another sample. Does your score remain the same, even if your audience changes? Do you have one style of writing, take it or leave it, no matter what the age or education of your reader? Using the Fog Index in the manner detailed below will help you answer such questions—and make any changes necessary.

A Self-Help Tool

One of the beauties of the Fog Index is that it can open the eyes of those whose writing tends to make others cringe. It is especially useful as a tool because it is self-applied and thus self-correcting. The offending writer merely shrugs in chagrin and makes the necessary changes.

The head of a large government agency and several of his staff once took my course at the same time. The boss was fond of big words and long, convoluted sentences, which overwhelmed his readers. His staff had tried without success to convince him that his writing was laborious and to get him to cut down on the polysyllables and shorten his sentences. Now here he was in my class, scoring his own writing: he applied the Fog Index formula and came out with a grade level of 18.

The boss smiled, a little embarrassed at himself, and on the spot vowed to use shorter sentences. In one stroke, the Fog Index did what the staff had been trying to accomplish for years. They sighed in relief.

It's simple. If the Fog Index is lower than your audience appeal, add a few compounds and semicolons and substitute more sophisticated vocabulary. If it is higher than you want it to be, cut down on the big words and vary the sentence length.

The norm for business sentences is no more than twenty-two words, which is somewhat restrictive; there will be times when a longer sentence is appropriate, and even fun, as long as you keep control. The last sentence in Exercise 12 has seventy-one words, and as you can see, the writer lost control of it; but it is possible, even powerful and hypnotic, to write a long sentence that works. Only, please, do not put two of them in a row. Apple Computer is well-known for its "user-friendly" manuals, often written entirely in active voice. Here is an example of a fifty-five-word sentence from the *Apple II Reference Manual* that works. Notice that the lead sentence has only eleven words.

The Apple Power Supply is a high-voltage "switching" power supply. While most other power supplies use a large transformer with many windings to convert the input voltage into many lesser voltages and then rectify and regulate these lesser voltages, the Apple power supply first converts the AC line voltage into a DC voltage, and then uses this DC voltage to drive a high-frequency oscillator.[6]

And here is a hundred-word sentence that I wrote just for fun to my niece Jennifer when her trip to meet her new baby cousin was canceled:

And, Jenny, if you can understand the peculiar logic of this, think of it this way: come September, our visit will be in front of you, not behind you; something still to look forward to, not to look back on; something exciting yet to happen; rather than a has-been, a will-be—and since your darling cousin Emily gets cuter by the day, she will be all that more the darling by the time you see her and all that less, I guess, had you seen her earlier than you will, had you seen her when you meant to. So there.

If you delight in long sentences, keep control, watch your parallels, use mostly monosyllabic words, and intersperse your long sentences with short, snappy ones.

The Fog Index in Reverse

The Fog Index is most useful when you apply it in reverse, that is, when you apply it not just to your own writing but to the writing you want to emulate. Apply the Fog Index in reverse, and aim to match the client you are dealing with, the prose level of the publication you are writing for. Determine the Fog Index of the classic examples of work in your field, whether that means award-winning ads or the speeches of Justice Holmes, and pattern your piece accordingly.

The advantage of using the Fog Index in reverse is the insight that it gives you into the writing of the audience you are addressing. This can be a powerful perspective. If you are an investment firm in New York with a major client in Minneapolis, your client may not meet with you personally and will often judge your compatibility by your written communication; it is important that that person see you as "speaking his language." Simple! Measure and match his Fog Index. If the client you are corresponding with writes to you with a Fog Index of 12, then your return reply is too inflated with 15 and too condescending with 6.

If you write for a particular periodical, you elevate (raise) your chances of appearing in print if you can ascertain (figure out) the Fog Index of your target market. (If their Fog Index is 10, use *raise* instead of *elevate* and *figure out* instead of *ascertain*.)

An attorney named Janet once told me this story: A client had sent her the draft of a letter, which she was to correct and send to a state agency. The letter contained irrelevant material, even some potential trouble-making statements. However, each time Janet rewrote her client's letter, it kept coming out sounding like a lawyer. Then she remembered the Fog Index I had taught her. She discovered that her client had a Fog Index of 8 but her revamped correspondence scored 12. She made the appropriate adjustments and rewrote the letter successfully. The client was very pleased ("It sounds as if I wrote it!" he said), and off to the state agency went the letter.

When you apply the Fog Index in reverse, be prepared for some surprises. An ad executive, for example, needs to know that ads have a considerably lower index than the magazines they appear in. Even if the reading level of the magazine's text is 11 or 12, people only want to pay 6- to 8-level attention to the ads.

I once challenged a group of lawyers to apply the Fog Index to the speeches of Justice Holmes. They were astonished to find that his speeches registered only 11.

The lesson is, we need not obfuscate in order to be classic.

CHANGING VERBS: INFLUENCING WITH INTEGRITY

Besides using the Fog Index in reverse, another, often dramatic way to establish a rapport with your audience is to be sensitive to their worldview and to the verbs and adverbs and adjectives that they tend to use as clues to that stance. People tend to take in information—and give it out—predominantly in the mode most comfortable to them, usually one of three: auditory, kinesthetic (active) or visual.

The theory of neurolinguistic programming (NLP) makes the point that you can judge a person's system by the verbs and "color" words he or she uses. For example, an auditory learner might write, "It sounds good to me," while a person who operates mainly from the kinesthetic stance might state, "I do not grasp your meaning." The visual approach can be recognized (*recognized* is a visual verb) by such expressions as "Let's take a look at it" or "That idea is not clear." If you want to be compatible with someone, notice and match the expression of his or her system.[7]

My mode is primarily kinesthetic and visual. I need to remember this and be sensitive to the auditory learners in my reading audience. In rereading chapter 3 of this book, I noticed quite a few kinesthetic words and changed some of them, particularly in the summation paragraphs, out of respect for my auditory readers.

The vision words or expressions in chapter 3 included *seen, overlooks, picture him, noticing, looking at, see it, insight, overview, sight.*

Before I made any changes, the auditory examples were few and far between: *tell us, speak, called, articulate.*

The kinesthetic expressions were embarrassingly abundant: *stands, emerged, uncovered, expanded, alive, examine, invite, share, provide, list, generate, offer, bundled, crackle, activate, enhance, encourage, kick sand in the face of, exercise, shine, show, aspire to, point to, provide a springboard, work things out, tap into, hold, touch, coming to grips with, opening doors, beaming, shaving, left behind.* All these in the first seven pages.

Originally this paragraph on p. 27 read

So, to see it in terms of right and left brain (or hemispheres) is another way of looking at the phenomena of Ariel and Caliban, of noticing that one part of your brain works best for ideas and one part helps with editing and structure. This division of labor is not strict, but it is a useful way of looking at. . .

To make it sound more auditory, I made five small changes.

So, to speak in terms of right and left brain (or hemispheres) is another way of expressing the phenomena that I have been calling Ariel and Caliban, of paying attention to the fact that one part of your brain works best for ideas and one part helps with editing and structure. This division of labor is not strict, but it is a useful way of talking about. . .

A later part was recast:

Whether you choose to call it Caliban and Ariel or think it sounds better to use the labels left brain and right brain, the important thing to realize is that what you have is there all along. To be whole-brained, you need only quiet down the noisy static side of you and listen to your own imagination.

If you're like me, you need to consider adding more auditory vocabulary to your overall text so that the auditory learners can hear you. If your worldview is auditory, be conscious of your verbs so your reader can see your point or feel at one with your position.

TRICKS OF THE TRADE

You have learned to eliminate the passive voice, cut down on your sentence length, vary your sentence meter, and match your parallels, but still your words lack luster. Here are two little tricks that professional writers use constantly to help give satisfying results.

1. The Echo

Instant professionalism: a verbal echo at the end of your piece that harks back to something you said in the beginning. Many newspaper columnists use this device in their daily work, and it never gets old. The trick is to take some word or phrase from your opener or from early on in your piece and echo it verbally at the end, often with a twist. Now that I have told you that trick, you are going to find it everywhere. (After writing this section, my heightened awareness found this device in five of six articles in the Columbia alumni magazine.) Before, you only knew that you were satisfied with a piece. Now you know why.

Echo endings presuppose that the beginning is also a summary. In my branching trees the opening and closing concepts are often on the same main branch, reminding me to give the reader a sense of having come full circle.

Remember the old college essays, in which you first stated what you were going to do in your blue book answer, then did it, and then tied it all together with "and thus we can see. . ." or something equally obvious?

You can be less transparent about it, but it is a good idea to tell the reader where he is going, how he will get there, and when he has arrived. Often the echo creates that unity effortlessly.

One of my students wrote a New Year's piece for the local paper with a nice use of the echo device. She had experienced a tragedy at Christmas: her opening paragraph told of the clean white calendar on her desk, symbol of her reluctance to get back into the swing of things after the holidays: "The unblemished calendar was tangible proof that I could remain home, within my comfort zone, secure and untouched by the outside world." Gradually, friends reach out to her and help her out of her cocoon, and at the end of the piece, she makes an entry on the calendar: to write and thank the friends and loved ones who were so supportive.

The line that you echo need not be right up front; sometimes the ending resonance can come from an idea buried in the middle of your writing. Columnist Dave Barry uses that technique all the time, often with his characteristic bizarre twist. One time, in the middle of a column, he accused his readers of having "no more media sophistication than a lung fluke" and then went merrily on with his topic. Four paragraphs later, he defined *lung fluke* as a parasite that can get into your lungs, and it was not until the end of the piece that he tied it all together by advising readers not to eat uncooked crab because they might pick up fluke larvae.

In chapter 3 I present the Garfield cartoon in the middle of the chapter and then echo it with a variation at the end: "Jon is wrong. Using both sides of the brain, cats *can* stand on their hind feet."

Well-written prose is like a fine piece of music that falls entertainingly on the ear, and the underlying principle of fine music is echo, repetition, variations on a theme. A repetition of the opening bars, often with a bar or two added, lets the listener know the piece has concluded. And there is a satisfying sense of having been part of it all.

2. End with Accent

Taking another analogy from music, it is often effective to end your piece on a downbeat. Openings are what catch the reader's attention and encourage him to read on; the ending is often what causes him to act on your words. Be forceful and dramatic in your last word, and your total communication will have more impact. The accented syllable is the one where the jaw drops: *sin cére,* or a single strong word such as *bráin.* Wherever possible, recast your sentence to arrange your words so that the last syllable is the accented one and you will leave an impression in the mind of your reader.

Ending accents are particularly favored by editorial writers and campaign speechwriters; that should tell you something. Rather than urging you lamely to "vote for this resolution," the forceful writer ends her exhortation with "This resolution deserves your vote!" It was no mistake that Patrick Henry did not go down in history saying, "Give me death, or give me liberty," nor is it surprising that they carried William Jennings Bryant out on their shoulders and nominated him for president when he roused the crowd with his impassioned ending accents: "You shall not crucify mankind upon a cross of gold."

Do you hear how less satisfying those endings might be had the authors chosen instead to finish with unaccented syllables?

Which moves you more to action: a letter that ends, "Give me a call if you have any problems," or one with more punch, "If you have any problems, give me a call"? Which sounds more forceful, more sincere? Which sounds like the kind of person with whom you want to do business?

I am happy to point out that, without contrivance, I managed to end many chapters of this book on a downbeat, in fact several times with a string of strong accents.

Chapter 2: *better they gét.*

EXERCISE 14: ACCENTED ENDINGS

Recast these sentences so that they end on an accented syllable.

1. Please feel free to contact me should you desire further information.
2. There are both legal and professional mandates for using this process.
3. Table 1 lists the free pamphlets available from national organizations.

STRIP MINING

Sometimes you have written a piece that does not hang together, but you cannot quite figure out the glitch. Strip mining to the rescue. I came upon this useful technique almost by accident, working with first-graders. When you are just learning to print, it is difficult to edit, because your ideas are so spread out that you easily lose sight of the relationship of your sentences to each other. One sentence can take up a whole fat-lined page and trail onto the next. My students were having such trouble editing that I knew we needed something smaller to manipulate. So I typed up their poems and stories line by line, each sentence or thought on a separate line, and then we cut them into strips. As an example, here is a poem about what it would be like to be ten feet tall, by a first-grader, Jason.

> If I were ten feet tall, I would put clouds in my pillowcase.
> I would climb the Empire State Building like King Kong.
> I could pick up that lady in my hand like King Kong.
> I would have the biggest ears in the world.
> I would be a basketball player.
> I could catch all the bugs in the world and throw them all away.
> I would be taller than anybody in the world.
> I would climb the biggest ladder in the world.
> I would climb that ladder up and out of the universe and I would
>   climb back down with thousands of stars in my arms.
> I would have the biggest arms in the world.
> I would have the biggest feet in the world.
> I would kick a ball up to Mars.
> I'd have the biggest house in the world.

Not bad for a six-year-old. Some nice images and ideas, and Jason was pleased because he had never written that much before. But he did not think it sounded like a poem. We laid out the strips on his desk, and I asked him to group like things together. So he put together the strips about the feet and the ears and the arms and then figured that if he had the biggest feet, arms, and ears in the world, he would porobably need the biggest house. He liked the line about the clouds in his pillowcase, so he decided to leave that first. Now he could see that the basketball player did not go with anything else, so he put it aside. He had not changed a word; he had simply rearranged what was already there, and left out one line. Now this is the way his poem sounded:

> If I were ten feet tall, I would put clouds in my pillowcase.
> I would have the biggest arms in the world.
> I would have the biggest feet in the world.
> I would have the biggest ears in the world
> > and
> I'd have the biggest house in the world.
> I would be taller than anybody in the world.
> I would climb the Empire State Building like King Kong.
> I could pick up that lady in my hand like King Kong
> > and
> I would kick a ball up to Mars.
> I could catch all the bugs in the world and throw them all away.
> I would climb the biggest ladder in the world.
> I would climb that ladder up and out of the universe.
> And I would climb back down with thousands of stars in my arms.

Now that's a poem!

You need not literally cut up your sentences into strips, although it is fun to manipulate your words that way: a simple and effective approach is simply to circle the key word in each sentence in a paragraph. Then you'll have 5 or 6 words to juggle around rather than 150.

At the beginning of this chapter, I used this method to help organize a paragraph that was not hanging together. Originally, it read

Remember, Caliban returns now at your invitation, as your guest, and so he comes back as your friend. Editing invites the left and logical side of your brain to return with you to your written piece and offer specific advice on improvement and rearrangement. The difference between this sort of editing and the premature edit voice is that, where before the edit voice put you down, now Caliban is ready to offer adult-to-adult suggestions on improving your writing.

Rather than manipulating 80 words to find the problem, I circled the key word in each sentence: *Caliban, editing* and *difference*. Now I could see that *Caliban* had to go in the middle because it was part of the whole, a category under the general heading of *editing*. I added "though" and rearranged the sentences to read

Editing invites the left and logical side of your brain to return with you to your written piece and offer specific advice on improvement and rearrangement. Remember, though, Caliban returns now at your invitation, as your guest, and so he comes back as your friend. The difference between this sort of editing and the premature edit voice is that, where before the edit voice put you down, now Caliban is ready to offer adult-to-adult suggestions on improving your writing.

EXERCISE 15: Strip Mining

Use a paragraph of your own writing or the one provided below. Circle the main words of each sentence to see the ingredient that does not fit, the new idea that is introduced without transition.

It was inevitable that the attempt should be made. The Canadian Opera Company in Toronto was the first to experiment with the idea of projecting a translation on a screen over the stage. A similar system was inaugurated by New York City Opera during their abbreviated 1982–83 season, with numerous additional major American and foreign companies quickly following suit. The translation being used in the current production of *La Traviata* was first devised at the suggestion of Francesca Zambello, a young, live-wire opera director who staged *La Traviata* during San Francisco's 1983 Fall Season.[8]

FALLACIES: ERRORS IN REASONING

"The problem," said Christopher Morley, "is to teach ourselves to think and the writing will take care of itself."

One of the most effective and permanent ways to insure that your writing flows logically is to be able to recognize fallacies in your own and other people's writing.Even if an argument appears reasonable, closer examination sometimes reveals a fallacy, that is, unclear thinking with an illogical conclusion. Recognizing fallacies forces you to stick to the issue without getting sidetracked. As I understand it, fleeing criminals, to throw bloodhounds off their track, would smear themselves with spoiled (red) herring to destroy their own scent, sending the search dogs down the wrong trail. In a broad sense, then, every informal fallacy is a "red herring," because it draws you away from the true issue and hooks you into considerations that have nothing to do with the matter at hand. Being aware of fallacies and knowing how to label them gives you a decided advantage in forming sound arguments yourself and in analyzing others' not-so-sound ones. This skill will sharpen your wit as well as your writing.

I recommend that you buy and enjoy a good logic book. One of my favorites, because it is not at all pedantic (it even includes cartoons), is *With Good Reason* by S. Morris Engel. Tony Buzan has a good chapter on fallacies in *Make the Most of Your Mind*, and S. I. Hayakawa's *Language in Thought and Action*, written in 1939 and now in its fourth edition, still serves well.

To arm you in the meantime, I have put together this short guide. I have cast my examples predominately in terms of parent-child dynamics, first, because we can all identify with that sort of relationship (even if you are not a parent, you once were a child), and second, because you can use this knowledge not only in writing but also in your verbal interactions with your offspring (or your boss, spouse, friend, banker, or the TV repairman).

Knowing fallacies will prepare you to write incisively and logically, using sound arguments or knowing when to employ rhetoric for effect and persuasion; you will also have an advantage in any argument and you will automatically become a more judicious listener and reader of politicians and the daily news.

INSANITY IS HEREDITARY: YOU GET IT FROM YOUR KIDS

I don't know why all the popular child psychology books don't include, as a matter of form, a chapter on logic. Whenever you need an example of a fallacy, count on a child to supply you with one. Listen.

1. Fallacy of Accent

Mother: Please don't leave your clothes on the floor, dear. Would you kindly pick up your jacket, and don't throw it there again.

Child: It's not my jacket, it's my coat.

The fallacy of accent deliberately or unintentionally places the emphasis on the wrong part of your sentence, leading you to argue a point that is not at issue. Or it gives weight to a minor aspect of your statement, clouding the more important issue. Movie advertisers often deliberately commit the fallacy of accent. The reviewer writes, "If they gave Oscars for poor acting and staging, this movie deserves an Oscar." The ad writer conveniently omits part of that sentence and announces on the movie page that ". . . this movie deserves an Oscar!" Fallacy of accent.

Kids love the fallacy of accent. When you tell them to stop banging on the table, they comply by banging on the wall, and when you ask "Did you tell your brother to stop spraying the hose at the house?" Sister comes back in sopping wet: "Yes, I told him."

And Lord Byron, when told that students at Cambridge were not allowed to keep dogs in their rooms, obeyed the rules and confounded the dean. He kept a bear.

2. Generalizations
(a) Hasty

The hasty generalization assumes a general principle on the evidence of a few examples.

Mother: We don't want you to go to the rock concert.

Teenager: But Maa-um, everybody is going! They all think you are so mean. You are the meanest mom in the whole world.

All three exclamations are oversimplifications—general statements based on insufficient evidence.

In writing, hasty generalization persuades because, based on a few examples, the writer implies that the application of the principle presented is widespread. In a letter to the editor of a local paper, a woman complained that this newspaper had no women's section; citing three major newspapers that did, she concluded that all papers of any note had a women's section.

(b) Sweeping

A sweeping generalization, called in Latin *dicto simpliciter*, reverses that scheme, taking a general principle and applying it broadly where it does not apply.

Daughter: You told me always to tell the truth, so I told the neighbors that you said their lawn was a disgrace to the neighborhood.

Another example:

Son: Everyone loves a joke, so how come the guys on the football team didn't laugh when we put itching powder in their uniform pants?

Again, it is a matter of oversimplification; here, based on an unqualified generalization where the general rule does not apply to the specific case. Sweeping generalizations are particularly dangerous when we use them to argue that what is true of a whole group applies equally to individual members of that group.

3. Personal Attack

An *ad hominem* ("against the man") attack directs attention away from the argument to the person making the argument. One type takes a direct, abusive shot by name calling: for example, criticizing the teacher instead of accepting responsibility for a poor grade, or calling you, the parent, unfair instead of examining the issue surrounding your decision. (See how fallacies overlap? "You are so mean!")

Another version of the *ad hominem* attack is called poisoning the well. Before the person has had a chance to present herself or her argument, this fallacy besmirches her reputation. It is a form of *ad hominem* because it goes for the jugular of the person rather than the heart of the argument.

Notice that the fallacy of poisoning the well often includes other fallacies to bring home its devious point.

High school student: Before you even go to see my teacher, I think you should know she has a reputation for being an airhead. Everybody hates her [hasty generalization]. Even the principal thinks she's weird [appeal to authority].

Yet another form of *ad hominem* is a fallacy that kids love; the Latin name for it is *tu quoque*. The name means "you also," and it is an attempt to discredit the argument by attacking the person presenting it because he does not "practice what he preaches." Here is an example of *tu quoque*:

Parent: I want this room cleaned, and I want it cleaned now. I wish you would keep it tidier.

Kid: You should talk. Your car [desk, briefcase] is always trashed out. Who are you to tell me to clean up my space?

Another example:

Father: Don't let your homework go until Sunday night, and get working on those term papers early in the semester. You get in trouble when you put things off until the last minute.

Teenager: You're telling me! And who's the one who waits until April 14th every year to do his taxes?

Lee Iacocca, in his bestselling autobiography, used a veiled *ad hominem* argument to discredit one of his opponents in the Chrysler bailout. He speaks at length of this congressman's manipulation of the media to turn people against a federal loan guarantee, and then takes what was, no doubt, an irresistible swipe. This same congressman, he reports, "the great defender of the American way of life, was convicted twice in the Abscam affair and sentenced to a term in jail. He lost the election, and went out in disrepute. . . .

"Poetic justice!" crows Iacocca.[9] Perhaps, but also, in terms of his argument, *tu quoque*.

Who the speaker is or how he lives his life is irrelevant to the soundness of an argument.

4. *Appeal to Authority*

Quoting an expert to lend credibility to an argument is known as an appeal to authority, or, in Latin, *ipse dixit* ("he himself said it"). It is a powerful persuader:

Teenager: Janet's parents let her go to R-rated movies. Tim's parents let him go to R-rated movies; even Margaret is allowed to go to R-rated movies, and you know how strict her parents are! Why can't I go?

The appeal to authority is one of kids' strongest defenses. You might be strongly against your son or daughter driving at age sixteen, for example, until, one after another, his or her friends drive up in their cars, and you start to weaken. This is an indirect appeal to authority: *their* parents (authority) think it is okay to drive at sixteen; what's wrong with you?

I see the appeal to authority as a teenager's strongest suit, even playing one parent against another.

Kid: (To Mom) Can I have a raise in my allowance? Dad says it's okay. (*Then to Dad*) Mom says it's okay to raise my allowance if it's okay with you.

Be wary!

In writing, it is often useful to quote other people to back up your own arguments. I do it myself quite often throughout this book. There is nothing intrinsically wrong with quoting experts for color and even support, but be careful that the argument stands on its own merits without the prop.

5. *Bifurcation*

A classic example of manipulation based on fallacies is the "either-or" fallacy, which overlooks a third option, "none of the above." The correct term for it is bifurcation, coming from the Latin *bifurcus*, meaning "two-pronged" (*bi* is the Latin prefix for "two"; *furca* menas "fork or branch"). It is the "either-you-help-me-with-my-homework-or-I-fail" type of argument, which excludes the alternative "Do your own homework." "If you don't buy me a car, I will be late for work every day" sidesteps at least two other possibilities: "Buy yourself a car" or "Get up earlier and catch the bus." "Let me get my ears pierced or I'll be a social outcast. None of the kids in school will talk to me." This last is also an appeal to pity (see below). Do not get trapped. Bifurcation forces you to choose between two alternatives when your choices are actually not so limited. You think you are in a bind, but you are not. Make the decision based on its own merits.

Advertisers often make use of bifurcation because it conveniently gives the consumer only two choices: the one, some dire consequence; the other, to buy their product. New York Air published an ad showing a cast-off wedding ring and a note from a wife who had run off with another man while her husband was on a business trip. How sad, when, "for just $25," he could have taken her with him. The ad concludes that this special fare is "cheaper than a lawyer."

6. *Appeal to Pity*

If all else fails, the *ad misericordiam* ("to mercy") argument, the appeal to pity, often sways.

Student: I hope you give this paper a good grade. I worked all night on it. I spent hours in the library doing research, and I even missed out on a family outing. That should be worth an A.

The fallacy of *ad misericordiam* plays upon your sympathy to divert your attention from the matter under examination. Let me off the hook because of how I suffer; be nice to me because I am in pain. Here's another example:

Child: When you won't let me watch TV on school nights, I feel out of it at school the next day. The kids laugh at me because they are all talking about the shows on last night and laughing together, and I'm not part of their fun. It makes me feel so lonely that I want to cry. Sometimes I do cry, when nobody is looking. I go into the bathroom or the coat closet and just cry because nobody likes me. Nobody wants to be friends with a kid who is not allowed to watch TV.

Before you get out the violins and the hankies, label this fallacy for what it is. Then, if you want to discuss limited weeknight TV viewing, the way is free for a clear-headed discussion.

7. *False Analogy*

False analogy compares two activities that are alike in insignificant and trivial ways—but dissimilar in significant ways—in order to attach the onus of one to the situation of the other. False analogy usually applies an emotion-packed simile to a less volatile one or tries to reduce the significance of a highly charged issue by comparing it to a mundane one. Children usually escalate the situation upward, and their use of false analogy is subtle and thus potent. It can be enough to throw you off balance. Once you discern how easily this sort of argument seduces you away from the issue at hand, you will be alert to it in other areas of your life and on guard against it in your own writing.

If your son accuses you of child abuse because you won't let him have candy before dinner, that is false analogy. Especially because child abuse is such an emotionally charged topic, the issue of candy now takes on a whole new coloration—if you allow yourself to be sidetracked. Learn to separate the emotion-packed issue from the reality and you learn an important rule of logic.

The archbishop of Dublin warned that if divorce became legal in Ireland, "Divorce would spread through Ireland like the radiation that started at Chernobyl and then covered all of Europe." This was a particularly potent image since, after the accident in Russia, radiation levels in Irish lamb had increased five hundred percent, and people were scared. But radiation spreads through indiscriminate fallout, and divorce is chosen or not chosen by people in control of their own lives.

Metaphors and similes are powerful tools for the writer; when you use such images, be careful that the connections are sound.

8. *False Cause*

The fallacy of false cause occurs when we confuse cause and effect, assuming that an event is the direct result of something that occurred previously, when no such connection has been established. In Latin, it is known as *post hoc, ergo propter hoc*; the name describes the fallacy ("after this, therefore because of this").

Superstitions are often examples of *post hoc*:

Walking under a ladder brings bad luck; I knew a man once who walked under a ladder—two days later, he fell down and broke his neck.

Sometimes we use false cause arguments in a humorous way, for example,

Carrots are good for your eyes and I can prove it. Have your ever seen a rabbit with glasses?

Yet, like all other fallacies, *post hoc* is also used, often unwittingly, in a serious context, for example: A high school student, suspended from school for using suggestive language in a campaign speech, sued the school for violation of his freedom of speech. He took the case to the Supreme Court and lost. In an article defending his position, he wrote:

My friend was subsequently overwhelmingly elected, vindicating my campaign tactics.

False cause reasoning abounds in advertising, suggesting some absolute connection between the product and a desired outcome. Computer ads often imply that doing well in school is tied in with having a home computer, and conversely, not owning one leads to flunking out. A paper products ad tells of a concerned mother who worries that her daughter can't concentrate because she is too fidgety. "I was shocked to find that harsh toilet tissue was the cause." And an ad for bran cereal explains that a mother should not be angry with her daughter for a poor report card: constipation is at fault. *Post hoc, ergo propter hoc:* all of these examples commit the mistake of erroneous causal connection. Sequence does not prove consequence.

It is fun to be able to call fallacies by name (and especially useful to have the Latin phrases handy), but what we are after here is raising your consciousness about the existence of fallacies and lapses in logic—in your own and other people's writing. Once you are alert to even a few, you will start to listen more sharply to any argument and sense the illogic in your own writing and thinking. If the fallacy you detect does not fall into one of these categories or you need more information in defining your terms, check *Make the Most of Your Mind* or *With Good Reason*.

FALLACIES AND THE CRITIC

Knowing about fallacies helps you to deal with the Critic, who constantly tries to throw you off the scent with a red herring or two— not in your writing but in his dealings with you, which are always less than straight. For example, when you are working on a piece of writing and the Critic beleaguers you with, "What took you so long?" or "You know you'll never amount to anything" or "This will never fly" or "You're gonna be shot down" or whatever, remind him that all of these complaints are irrelevant to the task at hand and, ultimately, irrelevant to the quality of the writing you are presently doing. Any tricks you learn in dealing with your kids' illogic or your own can serve you well in putting the Critic back in place.

C. S. Lewis once said that writing was like "driving sheep down a road. If there is any gate to the left or right, the readers will most certainly go into it." Keep on the straight and narrow in your thinking, and your writing will follow the same direct path.

CHAPTER 9

Going to the Movies: Creative Visualization and Writing

I learned. . . that inspiration does not come like a bolt, nor is it kinetic, energetic striving, but it comes to us slowly and quietly and all the time, though we must regularly and every day give it a little chance to start flowing, prime it with a little solitude and idleness.
—Brenda Ueland, *If You Want to Write*

The Five R's of whole-brained writing will make your task more relaxed and more profitable. The tips and techniques of editing will make your finished piece more polished. But didn't I promise I would also make writing fun, a glorious adventure, a mind-expanding experience? That is what this chapter is all about.

CREATIVE VISUALIZATION

Creative visualization is the technique of using your imagination to create images and feelings inside your head; it is a powerful way to tap into the message center of the right brain. Creative visualization is like going to the movies inside your own head. In today's world of high-priced entertainment, it is a handy talent to cultivate. Visualization is no longer an esoteric practice, reserved for Buddhist monks and California psychics. Now it is in the mainstream to see pictures in your head. It's even in *Time* magazine.

When the Americans who were held captive in Iran were relased, they told of overcoming the stress of 444 days in captivity through various strategies. One hostage mentally remodeled a whole house, nail by nail, board by board; another went, in his mind's eye, on the Orient Express and recorded mentally every detail down to the menu. According to *Time*, the State Department doctors at Wiesbaden, Germany, called these survival tactics "Going to the Movies" and considered them good devices for "warding off the helplessness that comes with captivity."[1]

Not only captives in Iran need to ward off feelings of helplessness, and, fortunately, you don't have to be behind bars to get a free pass to this theater. In fact, you are carrying around in your own head a very rich source of entertainment and inspiration, a huge 3-D screen to play out life's mysteries and messages.

This chapter is a whetstone to make you keen and eager to incorporate the skill of visualization into your life and to show you how to apply it directly to your writing. Using visualization, you can bring the perfect writing environment to wherever you are, picture your success scenario, get inside the head of the person driving the car in front of you on the freeway. You can become your favorite author or ask an authority for personal advice with editing.

FROM SPORTS TO SCHOOLS TO SNEAKERS

It is no secret that today's Olympic contenders not only have athletic coaches, they have mind coaches. A popular book like *The Miracle of Sports Psychology,* by James Pravitz and James Bennett, attests to the power of the mind in achieving sports goals. Visualization is an accepted part of today's sports world. San Francisco outfielder Jim Wohlford, speaking of baseball, put it eloquently: "Ninety percent of this game," he said, "is half mental."[2]

Schools are also discovering, to the delight of student and teacher alike, how the use of relaxation techniques and guided imagery improves comprehension and raises grades and self-esteem. Studies done by Dr. Beverly-Colleene Galyean (see her book *Mind Sight*) show that students taught their other subjects with visualization improve academically and are less unruly, less truant, more motivated, more secure. Not only the students but also the teachers find the classroom a more pleasant place to be: learning is easier, teaching is easier, and both are more fun when visualization or guided imagery is incorporated into the curriculum.

And it is happening all over the world. *Paris Match,* for example, quotes Micheline Frank, a Parisian teacher, who emphasizes that relaxation and visualization are not "the corollary of passivity." On the contrary, she asserts, these techniques make possible greater concentration of attention, alertness, and receptivity to learning.

Visualization is even good for your heart. Dr. George Sheehan, the famous running guru, after spending 195 pages of his book, *Dr. Sheehan on Running,* extolling the virtues of jogging for the physically fit, then tells of this interesting experiment done in Canada with heart patients. The study divided cardiac patients into two groups for postoperative care. The one group trained strenuously, running and exercising every day. Those in the second group, under the guidance of a psychiatrist, were put into a hypnotic trance, in which they pictured themselves running through a field, with the wind in their faces and oxygen filling their lungs going straight to their hearts. After one year the results in both groups were identical. Weight down, blood pressure down, less body fat, grip strength increased to an identical degree. EKG readings showed the same improvement.

So visualization is here to stay and can even cut down on the cost of your sneakers! To visualize, you don't need training of any kind. You needn't be an expert. Even if you are skeptical, it will still happen if you let it. Because it is there already inside of you.

PART OF YOU KNOWS THE ANSWER

Did you ever walk over, say, to a cupboard or a drawer and forget what you went there for as you stood in front of it? The interior monologue at such times usually goes something like this:

"Dumb me! What did I come over here for? I must be losing my mind. How dumb!"

When that happens to me now, I say instead, "Wow. What smart feet I have. They knew to come this way even though I can no longer articulate why I am here."

Then I take a deep breath, close my eyes in a satisfied way, and let the image of what I came to get cross back over my corpus callosum into words.

When we sit down to write, we are often at the stage of "knowing but not knowing," as Perl and Egendorf name it in their study of the process of creative discovery.[3]

"Knowing but not knowing" is that sense that you know what to say but do not know how to say it. Your feet were smart enough to get you to the desk. You knew enough to pull out the paper and pick up the pen. Now you must somehow, as the computer people say, "access" the nonverbal information that will tell you what to write and how to write it.

Listen to what I am saying here! It is very important. We have already seen in chapter 5 that attending to your nonverbal side, quieting down the static and listening to your inner self, will help you get in touch with your feelings about a particular writing project and what may be blocking you. What I am suggesting here is even more radical, more powerful. I am suggesting that the thought itself (in nonverbal form), the shape and direction, the whole piece that you know but do not know, the content as well as the context, can be discovered by this same pathway. And that is what this chapter is about.

The right brain sends messages in terms of pictures and feelings. *Attend* to those images and you will be rewarded with knowledge.

LET YOUR BRAIN WAVES DO THE WALKING

In the past, when I mislaid some object, I would frantically search every logical place for the missing item. I have been known to waste an hour or more in thankless rummage. Now, I take a deep breath, sit

still, and say calmly, "The right side of my brain knows where it is."
Often the place pops right into mind. If not, I mentally go through
each room of the house, each nook and cranny at the office. When I
inwardly arrive at the right corner, I actually see the item there or feel
a sensation inside me. Sometimes there is a heat radiating from that
spot (remember the game "Hot or Cold" we played as children?).
Sometimes the space seems to glow, or shout, or vibrate. Whatever the
signal, the sense of it is strong and definite.

Then I open my eyes, get up, and go for it. And there it is.

In preparing to write this chapter, I located a magazine article that
had been missing for four years, using the same approach. I found
the article in a crawl space under the stairs, in an abandoned desk
rack, in with old recipes, report cards, a summer aerobics schedule,
an old tape of Beethoven's *Eroica,* an opera program, an immunization
form, and a personality profile test, filled out and never sent in for
scoring. In other words, in with things that had no connection at all
with the article I was searching for, in a place it had no right being.
Yet the movies of my mind led me directly to it.

When you incorporate the movies of your mind into your writing, it
not only gives you a healthy and playful attitude towards words and
ideas; it also often supplies the missing links. Below are several exercises that tap into this reserve. Use your own imagination to come up
with others.

SET UP THE SCREEN, TURN ON THE PROJECTOR

You don't need any fancy equipment for creative visualization. In
fact, you already own the projector and some pretty sophisticated
camera equipment. You even have some footage in there already that
is waiting to be unrolled. All you need to do is quiet down inside and
let it happen. The *let* is integral to the process. Do not force the image
or come ready with expected responses. Be mindful not to reject
whatever comes, even if its usefulness is not immediately apparent to
you. *Let* it happen. *Let* the sense unfold, the "opening up" come
forward; *let* the meaning "pop" from the image.[4]

You might want to read some of the exercises below slowly into a
tape recorder in a monotone voice, then play the tape back with your
eyes closed and the lights low. Or have a friend read a section to you
in a soothing voice, or just close your eyes, relax, and trust yourself
to remember whatever part is important to you. I encourage you to
prepare your own scripts based on these suggestions.

EXERCISE 16: CHARACTER FORMATION

If you are writing fiction or doing character sketches of any kind,
learning to see the world from behind another's eyes is invaluable. But
even for those of you who are writing nonfiction business letters,

reports, or proposals, this exercise is a fun way to keep your movie apparatus in gear, to keep all that million-dollar equipment in good working order. As we will see below, it will also sharpen your wits in preparation for using a powerful editing tool: getting inside the head of the person who will read your stuff.

You could be sitting on a park bench or driving in the car. Pick a person in front of you and imagine what it might be like to experience the world from his or her perspective. Where did he just come from? Where is she going next? Tune into her mind: turn up the volume a bit so you can hear the concerns and worries, the mutterings. Sit down in the movie theater of his mind for a moment and watch the pictures on his screen. Do not force anything, just let the images and sounds come.

Here's an example of how it works. While driving through morning traffic down a busy commercial street in town, I saw two things almost simultaneously. One was a sign in front of a gas station. In large letters it read, "RED EYE IS BACK!" At the same moment, my eye caught a man standing at a bus stop, with his shoulders bent and his head down. He was wearing a bowler (true!) and carrying an umbrella, even though it was only overcast, not raining. He looked defeated and discouraged, as though he were facing yet another dreary day. Before I knew what was happening, the two images coalesced. I kept on driving, but inside my head was a new voice, not my own. It was husky and depressed.

"I wish I were Red Eye. Sure, he's got a foul mouth and drinks too much, but everybody loves him. He can get away with murder. Rough-hewn, but damn good. They love him. They put up a big sign when he comes back.

"Ha! Nobody cares whether I'm at work or not. Can you picture them putting up a sign for me?

"And Mildred! If I have one more fight with Mildred going out the door, I'm not. . . "

Mildred! That's when I hit the brakes. Who let Mildred in?

You get the idea. You see how easy it is.

By the way, I do not necessarily recommend that you make any attempt to verify your cinematic snooping. Several months after the experience described above, I was in that very gas station buying gas.

Said I, "I'd like to meet your mechanic, the one you call Red Eye."

The attendant looked at me queerly.

I continued. "A few months back, you put up a big sign when he returned. 'Red Eye Is Back' it said." I gave my shoulders a little self-effacing shrug. "I'd just like to meet the guy."

"Lady. There ain't no guy named Red Eye. Red Eye is the name of an oil. We've been out of it for awhile, and so we put up a sign when we got it back in stock. Sorry to disappoint you."

Ah well. But for all I know, the little man in the bowler *was* feeling down and *did* just have a morning spat with a wife named Mildred.

EXERCISE 17: THE SUCCESS SCENARIO

Maybe you have heard about, or even experienced, how visualizing something you want can help make it happen. This exercise is part of that fine tradition, with a twist. Here, you use the theater of your mind to enjoy the pleasure of a well-written piece, and—even more dramatically—to help create the piece that brings such joy. I call this the success scenario.

Quieten yourself in whatever way works best for you. In your mind's eye, picture whatever, for you, would be the success scenario of the piece you are currently working on. If you are a lawyer preparing a brief, it might be hearing the opinion of the court and knowing that you won. A playwright might picture the party at Sardi's with champagne and streamers and exclamatory reviews pouring in. A manager who has been having trouble with her staff might picture her ideas being implemented and everyone friendly and smiling. For myself, it is the autograph party with the lines going out the door, all ages patiently waiting to have a moment to talk with me, maybe the Phil Donahue show, a write-up in *Time* magazine. Success for you might be a big hoopla or a quiet thing. It might include crowds of people, lots of noise, or it may be simply one person you care about patting you on the back.

Larry, an attorney, wanted to write an article for the *New York Times*. He had a colleague at the firm who was always lording it over him, and Larry knew that an article in the *Times* would be a neat way to match wits. Larry's scene of success and its accompanying good feeling was very simple. First he got quiet, inside and out, slowed his breathing, relaxed his muscle tension, and then he imagined this same fellow coming over to his desk. "Larry, I saw your piece in this morning's *Times*." "It was nothing," Larry answers with a shrug.

So a success scenario does not require fanfare. The idea is to immerse yourself thoroughly in that scene. Be playful. Have some fun. Let the smile cross your face. Let the happy and satisfied feeling suffuse your whole body. Let the glow of success start from your toes and move right up to your head. Get giddy from the rush of it. Pay particular attention to what people are saying, all the wonderful comments about your job well done. Let your ears burn. Nod and smile and soak it up. You've worked hard for this moment, and you deserve to bask in it. Reach out and touch whatever is tangible—the desk, the chair, the hand to shake. Become part of that scene, and enjoy it for as long as you want.

Here comes the twist. After playing with your success scene for awhile, let the noise die down, the crowd dissipate, the colleague walk away, the TV talk-show interview end—not abruptly but in a pleasant, relaxed kind of way. The people are gone, but the residual good feelings of success are still with you. You are alone now but feeling fine. Shake your head in a gesture of pleased wonderment. And now—this is the fun part—turn your attention to the writing that has been getting such praise and accolades. Pick up the brief off the courtroom table, open the cover of your new book, look at the memo on your desk that had exactly the results that you wanted, and now, as you read it for the first time, copy it down.

Here's an example of how it worked for me. When I first designed the brochure advertising my writing workshop, I wanted it to double as a poster as well as a flier. That way I would be able not only to send it through the mail but also to post it around town and ask various companies and organizations to tack it up on their bulletin boards.

I sat in a quiet library, away from distractions, and tried again and again to write the opening copy. It wouldn't click. It got worse. I started to feel uptight, and I heard my Critic say, "This is a fine kettle of fish, Ollie. You plan to save others, and yourself you cannot save." My adrenaline was rising, my foot tapping, my fingers tightening around the pencil. I knew it was time for a relaxation break. Staying at my chair, I put down my pencil, closed my eyes, and took a deep breath. I became conscious of my breathing and thought that my breath was like a pump, breathing out any tension, breathing in peace and relaxation. I said that very phrase several times to myself: "Out with tension; in with peace and relaxation. Out with tension; in with peace and relaxation." Soon the words matched the reality.

In my mind's inner eye I found myself going up and down the avenue in the university section of town, posting my brochure in bookstores, cafés, and on kiosks. I was interacting with various people, and all of them were very complimentary about my brochure and my workshop.

"May I post this in your window?"

"Certainly. Sounds like an interesting workshop. I'd like to go myself. When is it?"

Soon, people were following me down the street—I was like the Pied Piper—stopping to read what I had posted, and asking me excited questions about my workshop and where they could sign up. I felt like a little kid at the zoo with a red balloon, skipping and happy. As I held the stapler in my hand, I could feel the rough texture of the kiosk and hear the satisfying clunk as the staple penetrated the wood where many millions of staples before had sunk their metal teeth. Other posters vied for visual attention, but my poster stood out, almost glowed. It beckoned and enticed. The crowds were jostling with each other in a friendly way, all wanting to read about this wonderful workshop.

"Where can I sign up?"

"May I have another copy of that brochure for a friend?"

"This is dynamite. Count me in."

"Just what I've been waiting for."

"Tell you the truth, it was your opening paragraph that caught my eye."

That last comment made me curious: How did the winning paragraph read? I resisted the temptation to look at it; I wanted to bask some more in the stunning results. I was having fun. Anyone looking over to me in my carrel in the library would have seen a totally relaxed person with a blissful smile.

I waited until the crowds dispersed a bit and then quietly tacked my last brochure over the "Post No Notices" stencil on a poster-covered fence.

Now I stood back from it a moment, and this time I read it. I read the words that were creating such a positive response, read the opening hook that captured such attention. *As I read it, I wrote it down.*

Professional writers call it writer's block, but panic before a blank page is not exclusive to writers who are professional. Writing anxiety can immobilize anyone: business executives behind in correspondence, students struggling over term papers, lawyers laboring over legal briefs, nurses or social workers dreading report deadlines. People with writing apprehension have been known to let it determine the paths of their lives, choosing majors in college, and later jobs, that have few writing demands. Some let it limit their earning and advancement potential. Or those who have been writing successfully for years suddenly find their creative juices run dry. Others have stories inside them that they want to tell, but they just can't get the words out. This workshop is for all of you.

Perhaps you've even taken some courses, or read some books that have given you hints and tips on breaking out of this syndrome. This workshop does more than give tips and strategies to fight the immediate problem—it arms you with tools to be your own best strategist from now on. Discover why you can't write on those days when the writing drags, and why you can write on those days when everything flows. Armed with that information, your writing will be productive for the rest of your life.

If you ever hesitate in writing, this workshop is for you.

It was almost cheating. The words were printed there so clearly before me. I could actually see them, not handwritten on a yellow pad but printed on a page with my twisted-pencil logo blown up on the side. I simply surreptitiously copied them down.

This approach is a wonderful catalyst, but do not think that just because you've seen it in print it does not need improvement. I needed to emend my brochure copy: a dangling participle, the enemy of the people, had crept into the last line of the second paragraph, and that line needed to be ruthlessly rearranged. I changed it to "Armed with that information, you can be a productive writer for the rest of your life." Then I took out the mixed metaphor of "arms you with tools;" in doing that, corrected as well the redundancy of "arms" and "armed."

So your mental manuscript starts out with a burst of energy and playfulness, but like everything else you write, it undergoes the same scrutiny of the Five R's of whole-brained writing. Visualization is actually just another way of doing Step 1.

There are many other dramatic examples of this creative construction. Chuck Loch, in an article called "How to Feed Your Brain and Develop Your Creativity,"[5] tells of a songwriter who "used to see the titles of his unwritten songs listed on a mental jukebox. In his mind, he would drop in a quarter and sit back and listen to his song, copying it down as he heard it played."

Or take the example of the senior executive of a large shipping company who told me that he was having a dreadful problem with phone etiquette in his firm. He had sent out many memos, most of them curt and authoritarian in tone, but they did not get the kind of response he wanted. In fact, they made things even worse. Most of his memos began with phrases like "It has come to my attention. . . " and "Unfortunately, it is once again necessary to inform you that. . . . "

Not only did the phone problem persist, but he had created a tension among his employees that ran counter to his usual management style and disturbed the atmosphere he liked to maintain in his company.

While taking my workshop, he played around with the success scenario of the perfect memo. He felt himself back in his office, even noticed what he was wearing and saw the items and papers on his desk. Mostly, though, he was conscious of a feeling of well-being, a sense of contentment around the office that he had missed. People were courteous without being stiff; there was a genuine feeling of camaraderie and goodwill. It was a nice place to be. There was almost a perceptible hum in the office of people working together. In his mind's eye he stayed with that feeling of satisfaction and went about his own work eagerly, knowing that all the people around him were working hard and happily. He told me later that it resembled the unexpressed sense of harmony you feel when the whole family is working on projects in different corners of the house. He still didn't know how it had happened, and in some ways it didn't matter. He was just enjoying the aftermath.

Then his eye strayed to a copy of the morning memo on his desk. He read:

We are all part of a family here, and as any growing family knows, there are times when we need to pitch in together to make changes necessary for the betterment of the whole.

As he read it, it pleased him. He wrote it down.

He could hardly wait to get back to his office and make that memo a reality. He made a few minor changes in what he had copied from his mind's memo and sent it out to the people in his company the next day. Guess what? The results were almost exactly as he had envisioned them. Once again, his company was a pleasant place to work, and an almost tangible team spirit prevailed.

EXERCISE 18: CARRY YOUR PERFECT WRITING ENVIRONMENT WHEREVER YOU GO

How many times have you said, "I could write *if only. . . ?*" If only I were someplace else, free from distractions. If only I could be in a room without clutter, without fingerprints. Or are you like the boss who tells me that she always brings her writing home, even though it irritates her husband, because she does her best writing outside the office? Save your marriage—and your sanity!

I remember a time in Newport when I wrote so fluently, so much, that I couldn't stop writing—it was a supportive atmosphere, free from distractions, free from pressure and responsibility. I wrote and wrote and wrote. I wrote so much that I even took the pad into the bathroom with me. I got up in the middle of the night and started writing. I was all charged up with a "Here-we-go! Don't-stop-now!" kind of energy and excitement. Ah! Where did that energy come from? It came from inside *me!* So I can re-create it anywhere, bring that space and that energy to my computer room, to my office, to my dining room table.

In *Sadhana* Anthony de Mello speaks of the mystic's ability to bring the past into the present by going in and out of the experience, each time noting what changes occur. Let's say that you did your best writing on the beach in Atlantic City or that time you were visiting the people with no children in Denver and the walls were white and had no handprints. That energy, that ability to write came from inside YOU! And it is yours for the asking to recapture it. Here's how.

First, relax. Get into a comfortable position. Close your eyes. Take a deep breath. Start with the top of your head and gently relax every muscle, working your way down to the very soles of your feet. Once your body is relaxed, go in your mind's eye to your perfect writing environment. In that quiet center, see yourself writing and writing, the energy and heat coming off the very page, burning a hole in the paper. It is wonderful to write like that. It is energizing and exciting. And the writing is good—clear and lucid, and so human. Keep on writing. What does it feel like to be writing like that? How does it feel inside of you, in your gut, in the center of your being? How does your hand feel, what is your head like? Can you locate the feeling in a part of your body? Can you taste it, smell it, touch it?

Now, return to the room you are in, but not abruptly or fully. How does it feel to come back to this room? Are you cold? Do you have less energy? Is it demoralizing, draining, sapping your vitality? Do you notice even a slight carryover from your perfect writing state? Stay with that feeling for a moment. Then return to the fullness of your perfect environment. Play with it, move back and forth, until you sense a strong transference of the vibes of the past scene into the present.

EXERCISE 19: BECOME THE AUDIENCE

François Rochaix, a stage director, says that the last thing he does before the final production of an opera is become like the audience to test his design:

I do all I can to prepare for a production ahead of time, with reading and thinking and working with designers. But once the rehearsals begin I have to turn into someone else too. Without forgetting what it is I set out to do, I must become like a member of the audience, see it all as they will see it, so that I can help the singers know what is the effect that we make. What they bring to it now is what matters most, because it is only that which makes it all come together and come to life.[6]

Even though editing is basically a left-brained task, the right can contribute in its strength to make the task easier, more pleasant, more fun—and more effective. Remember the goal in writing on both sides of the brain is to get that corpus callosum crackling, and this exercise is one sure way to make that happen.

In chapter 8 I told you to become the audience before editing and read your piece as though you were seeing it for the first time. Creative visualization builds audience awareness in a profound way. I suggest that you have a little fun with this. Using the approach outlined in Exercise 16, get inside the mind of your intended reader. You might know specifically who that person will be (such as a difficult person to whom you have drafted a tactful letter), or it might just be a generic type.

So quiet down inside. Take a deep breath. ("Your breathing is your greatest friend," says de Mello, quoting a Tibetan sage. "Return to it in all your troubles, and you will find comfort and guidance.") Close your eyes, relax, and bring to mind the person who will be reading your piece.

Think of where he might be when he receives this letter, what she might be doing right before this memo crosses her desk. Is the judge reading your brief in his chambers; has your boss gone through a stack of infuriating papers and finally worked her way down to your proposal; is the editor up to here with queries and now opening up yours?

Notice the body posture and the expression on the face. What insights do these clues give you into how that person feels? What concerns occupy her thoughts? Is the phone ringing off the hook, has she just had another cup of coffee or an upsetting encounter with another employee? What kind of effect are you going for? Get as much into the mind and the environment of that person (your reader) as possible. Put the reading of your piece in context—in the same context it will be received in. Does the reader seem hostile to your subject? If so, it is even more important to play with this projection for awhile. Become the audience. What is it like to be him? What is it like to be her? Stay with that image, using all of your senses: see, hear, taste, smell, and touch the world with your reader's eyes, ears, nose, mouth, and fingers. Now, inside his head, not your own, pick up your writing with his hands, read it through with her eyes, feel their visceral response to it.

Is it "Oh, here's _____ . I always like to read her byline"? Or is it "I'm mad already just seeing the return address" or perhaps "Wouldn't you know, another letter from the boss finding fault with me again—brace yourself"?

Now read your piece. What happens? Are you impressed? Are you entertained? Are you insulted, or pleased? Or confused? Does the writing keep you moving along in a pleasant pace, or are you bored and tempted to put it aside and come back to it later? Are you confused, angry, upset? Does a word strike you as harsh? Mark in the margin all the places where it pings.

Move on to Steps 4 and 5 of the Five R's of whole-brained writing, and finish your editing using some of the tips from chapter 8.

EXERCISE 20: CONFER WITH EXPERT

Once you learn, using any of the forms above, to tap into your creative center, ask for a guide to meet you there. This guide might arrive in the form of a friend or an animal or someone famous in your field. I like to invite John Fowles, Geoffrey Chaucer, or Jane Austen to help me edit. Jane Austen, in particular, was a great friend to me during the editing stages of this book. At one point, when I was feeling overwhelmed by the sheer amount of work ahead of me, I took a breather. I moved to a comfortable chair (my Ruminating Chair, in fact). What would Jane Austen do? I wondered. I know she reworked her novels meticulously right up to her death. I slowed my breathing, letting relaxation flow over me. In my imagination, I was walking along a forest path, an actual spot that is a favorite comforting place. There are majestic evergreens all around, but it is not a closed or confined place, nor is it dark and forbidding. The trees line a path that beckons forward to an expansive vista. The sun was streaming along that path in an invitational way, and it was from this clearing that Jane Austen came forward to greet me. She hailed me warmly. She was dressed in an Empire gown of antique ivory hue, with an umber sash beneath the bodice. She was business-like but kind.

She took me by the elbow and, demonstrating for me even as she led me to follow, she said, "Henriette. Like this. Look at your feet. One step. Good. Now the next step. Good. Now another. Step by step. You can do it. One step at a time. Come on—" (still urging me on by my elbow)"—I'm with you now. Step by step."

I went back to my work renewed, and instead of keeping the giant mass of raw unworked pages of the complete manuscript on my desk, I put the bulk of it aside and took one chapter at a time, one page at a time. Whenever I faltered, I said, "Look at your feet, not ahead. One foot after the other. Come on, one foot—that's it—after the other." It was good advice. I am grateful to Jane Austen for passing it on.

Another time, I invited John Fowles to meet me in the library of my mind, and when he showed up, he had brought a friend, Tony Buzan. Tony was exactly the fellow I needed to talk to then, so I was flabbergasted and delighted that John had brought him along.

Maureen Murdoch, in her book *Spinning Inward,* tells of using a technique with children that she calls "Skill Rehearsal with a Master Teacher." The results are astonishing. "Children report invoking Pelé to improve soccer kicks, Haydn to tutor piano, and Mark Twain to put some humor into their writing," she relates.[7]

Invite me, if you don't mind your work being a bit cavalier in spots. I'll be glad to help you in any way I can.

Chuck Loch, in an article mentioned earlier, suggests an intriguing variation of this exercise. His idea is to "imagine yourself going back in time, back to another lifetime when you were a famous writer of the past." The more vivid you can make the scene, the better. "Feel yourself in that writer's study, sitting at that writer's desk, taking pen in hand, writing a 'lost' manuscript." Then all you need to do is write the words along with the celebrated author and produce your own masterpiece. Loch gives several examples of students who had successfully employed this playful technique, and he once told me that he uses it in his own writing.

These ideas, and others like them, work, according to Loch, because they "generate strong synchronized brain waves," which emulate the pattern, confirmed by research, of the electric wave activity in the brain during peak moments of creative inspiration. Such exercises "reestablish the balance between both sides of the brain. They recreate the brain wave pattern for creative inspiration in which all parts work together."[8]

In other words, you are writing on both sides of your brain.

A PARTING WORD

We have a parting expression in our family that I would like to share with you. When our children have studied hard for a test, or worked long hours on a dramatic recital, or prepared carefully for a presentation of any sort, we do not send them off with the usual "Good luck!" They have worked hard for whatever triumph awaits them, and their work needs to be acknowledged and validated. They have used part of their brain that was theirs to claim. Luck has nothing to do with it.

Working through the exercises in this book took dedication and commitment on your part, and whatever was revealed was talent you had in you all along. The world of fluent, productive, on-time writing is at your command. It's already yours. It's already there.

The human mind has all kinds of software we are not using, simply because no one ever showed us how. Reclaim your birthright! And when you do, give yourself tremendous credit. Give yourself a big pat on the back. Send yourself off with a big smile on your face and a spring in your step. You are wonderful. Quite brilliant. Genius class. And it was there all along. What a marvel you are!

Send yourself off with these words of praise and acknowledgment ringing in your ears. Before you began reading this book, you had enormous talent that you brought to the work. Now you know how to get at it. It is only the beginning. A time capsule of internal combustion is planted inside you. Go for it, 100 percent!

Good skill!

Whole-Brained Spelling

I have a friend who has taught spelling in high school for twenty years. He begins each semester by saying, "Spelling is a very important indicator. If you consistently, assuredly spell correctly 100 percent of the time, it is an indication that you are an excellent speller. On the other hand, if you consistently misspell words, or do not trust your spelling, it is an indication that you are not an excellent speller."

In other words, good spelling has nothing to do with being "smart" or "dumb"; in fact, many great thinkers have been terrible spellers. So first get rid of any moral judgments you might have about yourself if you are a poor or fair-to- middling speller. Good spelling simply has to do with your visual memory and how brightly you can tune it up, and that is a skill that everyone can master. You are not doomed, you are not "dumb." You need not resign yourself to your fate or waste time looking up words. And you do not have to go back to school all over again and get ready for weekly spelling tests.

Why improve? First, for confidence and self-esteem, and for the time saved from looking words up. Also, an improved visual memory is useful for other things as well. If you get in shape for running, the increased leg strength will help you in bicycling, too. Visual spelling raises your awareness of the importance and effectiveness of visual memory.

THE RIGHT BRAIN CAN HELP THE LEFT BRAIN TO SPELL

Contrary to what we may have learned in school, "sounding out" words is the worst way to learn spelling, because words in the English language are often not spelled the way they sound. Neurolinguistic programming (NLP) researchers contend that spelling is best learned by using our visual memory rather than by the more traditional auditory approach. The better your visual memory, the brighter your images when you picture a word, and the better the speller you will be.

A "kinesthetic" response often goes along with a good speller's visual memory—you feel a "punch" in the stomach or a tightness in the jaw when a word is misspelled. A misspelled word will jar, even pain, a good speller, which is why some of us have been known to correct signs in public places: a store announcing in window-wide letters that "seperates" are on sale; a small sign by the register that warns "reciepts are necessary" for return of items. Correcting such errors, or pointing them out to salespeople, alleviates the pain, and that is why we do it. We are not trying to be obnoxious or self-righteous; we simply do not feel comfortable when we see a misspelled word, and we need to readjust our comfort level.

VISUAL MEMORY

According to NLP research, the "visual memory box" is indicated by eye movements that, for most people, move up and to the left. To confirm that, you can watch the eye movements of someone recalling something. In fact, NLP encourages teachers to put any information that they want students to learn in the upper left corner of the board, or the majority of students will not even see it. If this is true for you, place the spelling word you want to remember, or are tired of looking up, on the wall to your upper left. Look at it long and hard. Notice the curves and the straight parts. Notice particularly the first and last letters, and any small words within the word. Take a mental snapshot of it; blink your eyes like the shutter of a camera, hold your eyes closed for several seconds, and then read the word off the inside of your eyelids.

If you hear yourself spelling out the word internally (in other words, exercising your auditory skills), then stop and concentrate instead on taking a picture of the full word or segments of syllables. Let your eyes trace up and down the outline of each letter silently.

When you feel ready, cover the word with a white strip of board the same size as your word strip, and, while looking at the same space, "read" the word out loud off your visual memory screen. Does it feel right? Test yourself by writing it out on paper. Now take down the cover board and check it. If you were mistaken in a letter or if you felt unsure about a syllable, mentally exaggerate or color that letter or syllable this time, or make it vibrate. Click. Click. Take more pictures. Cover the word again. Now spell it backwards and forwards (that's easy if you are "reading" it, right?) Check it. Any letters incorrect or out of order?

Keep doing this until you "see" the word on the blank white board.

KINESTHETIC MEMORY

To implant the spelling in your kinesthetic memory, write it in the air, using your whole arm, with two fingers extended. Write it on the palm of your hand, using one finger. While you do your morning exercises, recite the word in rhythm to the beat of your jumping jacks or pushups. Sing a song, a tune you like, and in place of the lyrics, spell out your word. Sing it out loud in the shower or while driving the car.

Now the word is solidly yours, forever, and you can retrieve it instantly by picturing its vibrating letters on the wall, feeling it on yor arm, singing it along with a favorite song.

You can use any of these approaches by itself or all of them in conjunction to dramatically improve your spelling prowess.

The beauty of whole-brained spelling is that after a short while, it becomes a part of you, and you will find all of your spelling improving. By taking the time to work with only a few bothersome words, you become attuned to other words that you have not subjected to this method.

WORDS TO WATCH OUT FOR

If spelling is a crisis problem for you or one of your children, you may be pleased to know about an intriguing book, *The Reading Teacher's Book of Lists*,[1] which provides, among other lists, computer words, science words, and the "1,000 Most Common Words in the English Language." The authors claim that this last list makes up about 90 percent of all written material.

The Book of Lists also contains a section on "Spelling Demons"; words frequently misspelled by students. Of the 392 words listed, I have selected 210 that also plague adults, and I have added a few more that seem to crop up often in the papers I review for companies. Skip the ones that *look* clearly right to you. Put the others on strips of paper. Have someone hold them and flash them for you, or mount them on the wall and then follow the steps outlined above to implant them firmly in your visual and kinesthetic memory.

It is great to get your kids involved in this, because it will help them while helping you. Have them check the list themselves, and help them make up their own strips. The whole activity will be less threatening if you are also doing it.

MOST COMMONLY MISSPELLED WORDS

absence
acceptable
accommodate
accustom
ache
achievement
acquire
across
adolescent
advantageous
advertisement

advice
against
aisle
a lot
all right
alphabetize
amateur
analyze
annually
anticipated
apparent
appreciate
arctic
arguing

argument
arrangement
athlete

bargain
belief
beneficial
benefited
breathe
Britain
bury
business

calendar
category
cemetery
certainly
chocolate
choose
cite
commitment
comparative

concede

conceive
condemn
congratulations
conscience
conscientious

conscious
controversial
controversy
council
criticize

definitely
definition
descendant
describe
description
desert

dilemma
diligence
dining
disastrous
discipline
disease
disperse
dissatisfied

endeavor
effect
embarrass
emigrate
enough
environment
especially
exaggerate
exceed
except
exercise
exhausted
existence
experience
explanation

fascinate
fierce
formerly

forty
fourth

gaiety
gauge
grammar
guarantee
guidance

height
heroes
hypocrite

incredible
interest
interrupt
intersperse
irrelevant
its

jealousy
judgment

led
leisurely
license
lieutenant
listener
lose
luxury

magnificent
maneuver
marriage
mathematics
medicine
mere
miniature
miscellaneous
mischief
moral
muscle
mysterious

necessary
niece
noticeable
numerous

occasion

occurred
occurrence
occurring
opinion
opportunity

paid
parallel
paralyzed
particular
performance
personal
personnel
pleasant
politician
portrayed
possession

possible
practical
practice
precedent
preferred
prejudice
prepare
prescription
prestige

prevalent
principal
principle
privilege
probably
procedure
proceed
profession
professor
prominent
pursue

quiet

receipt
receive
recommend
referring
renowned
repetition
restaurant
rhythm

saucer
seize
sense
separate
sergeant
shining
similar
sincerely

sophomore
stationary
studying
substantial
subtle
succeed
succession
supersede
surprise
susceptible

technique
their
there
thorough
though
thought
through
tragedy
transferred
tremendous

unnecessary

vacuum
valuable
vegetable
vengeance
villain
visible

waive
weather
woman
wrench
write
writing

yacht
your
you're

Even more effective than consulting ready-made lists is generating your own personal list of spelling demons. Since they are demons, I call my list the Spellhole.

I keep a running tally in the back of my Progress Log. (I could never remember whether *occurred* had two *c*'s and two *r*'s or one *c* and one *r*, and *fascinate* always looked funny.) I jot down any words that annoy me, especially the ones that I look up in the dictionary because they do not "look right" and then find to my frustration that I spelled right in the first place. I keep a stack of paper strips, 8½ × 2¾" (a standard 8½ × 11" sheet cut into quarters), and a white cardboard "cover," the same size, in my top desk drawer. Once a week, I take the list from my log, print each word on a separate strip, and go through the steps outlined earlier until the word is solidly at home in my visual memory.

After a while, just to show off, you will want to test your new-found acuity and flex your mental muscles. So throw in a few of what the *Book of Lists* authors call "wise guys" words, like these:

pneumonultramicroscopicsilicovolcanoconiosis (lung disease caused by inhaling silica dust)
floccinaucinihilipilification (action of estimating as worthless)[2]

Or, two of my favorites:
triskaidecaphobia (fear of the number thirteen)
pachycephalosaurus (thick-headed dinosaur with a minute brain; hence, a large, dim-witted person).

You will be delighted to find that, once put in your visual memory, these words are as easy to recall as is, for example, knowing for all time that *occurred* has *two* *r*'s and *two* *c*'s.[3]

Writing on Both Sides of the Brain with a Word Processor

Writing with a word processor is a whole-brained experience. In the beginning, when you first get your computer, you need to take a left-brained, logical approach and follow the sequence of steps. But the longer you continue to approach it as a left-brained task (the way the computer manuals want you to), the more frustrating it becomes. Finally, you let go and recognize the computer for the truly right-brained, spontaneous, and playful tool that it is. You burn the manual, or you at least decide that reading it sequentially thwarts your efforts to be friends with your machine.

The computer is very literal, but any successful handling of it needs to be intuitive. Knowing this has helped me out of many a snag. When things go awry, I say, "What does the computer think I asked it to do?" and the answer gets me directly to the heart of it.

Many people exclaim new fluency when they use a word-processing program, and then give the computer the credit for their prolific output. *When it comes to words, it's a matter of who's to be master, that's all.* The same rule applies to computer-generated words. You are the one thinking up the words. So the question is, what can your new fluency with a computer tell you about the way your brain functions? What can you learn about yourself and how *you* operate that will transfer over to writing away from the computer? (Hint: it has to do with the Critic.)

Maybe it is as simple as the freedom of suspending judgment, either because of your computer's delete function, which gives you the freedom to write junque, or perhaps its ability to move blocks of text around, which gives you permission to write nonsequentially. Maybe it is the sense of proliferation you get as you watch a high-speed printer reel out page after page of copy. There's a healthy sense of abundance here, a secure "there's-more-where-that-came-from" feeling that helps immeasurably in editing.

These are useful points to know about yourself and what works best for you. William Zinsser, in *Writing with a Word Processor*, reveals that his process of writing, even with a computer, still includes editing as he goes along, so that's what works best for him. His style is smooth and invitational; I envy his results, if not his approach.

Comparing Zinsser's process to that of Donald Murray is a lesson in differences. Personally, I am of the Donald Murray school. I love his concept of writing as the "moment of surprise" that needs to be celebrated and anticipated. That is the moment at which the writer learns what he did not even know he had to learn. "Writers are, like all artists, rationalizers of accident," says Murray. "They find out what they are doing after they have done it." Murray suggests that writing is best accomplished when we go at it with "this purposeful unknow- ing, for writing is not the reporting of what was discovered, but the act of exploration itself."[1] The freedom of the word processor lends itself brilliantly to this pleasurable discovery, this playful planned spontaneity.

Dr. Peter Scharf raises the provocative question "Will writing on a word processor change the *aura* of books, change the *smell* of a good book?" I think not, as long as we remember who is in charge. The humanity that comes through in any good writing will be there whether it pours forth from an Olivetti or an Apple.

USING THE IDEAS IN THIS BOOK WITH A WORD PROCESSOR

Many of the ideas in this book adapt easily to word processing.

• Rapidwriting, of course (especially if your software allows easy deletion), and an electronic Progress Log are two of the more obvious applications. To duplicate the "Invisible Ink" exercise of chapter 2, turn off the screen before you enter ideas into your computer. It will bring home to you exactly how much you let the edit voice prematurely interfere with your copy, because the temptation will be so strong to turn the screen back on and bring the little green or amber characters back so you can dicker with them. Resist the impulse, and welcome instead the powerful experience of expressing yourself without pre- judgment. If your Critic is particularly strong at any given time, this is a trick you can pull out of your bag of them to instantly turn the proverbial "blank page" into your ally. You can of course go on like this indefinitely, but I recommend a minimum of ten minutes for all the reasons addressed in chapter 2. When you have finished this playful input, turn on the screen with a jolt of pleasure from having such a plethora of words magically and instantly appear before you, ready to edit. (By the way, I composed this paragraph using the blank screen approach.)

• It is also possible to keep on each disk such handy files as B4PRO (Before Procrastination), which already lists for you the questions suggested in chapter 6 for the BP entry. Then, if you find yourself procrastinating, call up the file right into the middle of your text, answer the questions, and carry on.

• You might want also to set up a file that keeps a running tally of words you need to be reminded to incorporate into your writing. In my case, I call the file Auditory, since I need to remind myself to use more auditory vocabulary. Periodically, I add new words to this file, especially if I come across useful additions in my reading of auditory authors. When I come to final editing of a piece, I call up this file to provide suggestions for substitutions. If you are an auditory learner, you might want to create a Visual or Active word file.

• I have also created a spelling file, which I use to flag any words I need to verify. If I have any doubt of a word, I add that word to my list of spelling demons. I date my waterloo words and, once a week, print the file and copy each word onto strips for visualization, as detailed in appendix 1. Then I can erase the file and start anew each week or, for my own satisfaction, create a back-up file that retains all the once-problem words, so I can note how far I have come. I keep a fresh file for my weekly words.

• More sophisticated programs are available that will help you diagram in a free-flow pattern similar to branching, and there are programs that will help you edit, alerting you to passive voice and clutter in your prose. There are even programs that will electronically check your Fog Index and give you the grade level of your audience.[2]

And, of course, any of the exercises in this book could easily be used *in conjunction with* a word processor. Branching and computers, for example, work hand in hand. Branch out all the points you want to cover on a sheet of paper before you start, and simply keep that branched outline next to your monitor as you work. Many students tell me that preparing that single sheet before beginning work on the word processor has expedited their writing considerably. Branching does some of the "cut-and-paste" work for you in advance by establishing a pattern for your random thoughts.

No matter how many fancy programs you find, no matter how wonderful you believe your computer to be, never lose sight of the fact that the function of the computer is to help you do faster what you already do well. When you ruminate, when you rapidwrite, when you revise—whether with paper and pen or at a keyboard—you are busy processing words in the ultimate and best word processor of all, the human mind.

Notes

CHAPTER 1: FROM PANIC TO POWER: MASTERY OVER THE WRITTEN WORD

1. Carl Sagan, *The Dragons of Eden: Speculations on the Evolution of Human Intelligence* (New York: Random House, 1977), 16.

CHAPTER 2: THE HAIR OF THE DOG THAT BIT YOU

1. Thanks to Donald Murray, professor at New Hampshire University, for telling me of Pliny's words. For Prof. Murray's own line about the unexpected, or, as he calls it, the "moment of surprise," see Appendix 2.

CHAPTER 3: RIGHT BRAIN/LEFT BRAIN: WHAT'S IT ALL ABOUT?

1. To my mind, one of the best of these books is an unbiased compilation of the research called *Left Brain, Right Brain,* by Sally P. Springer and Georg Deutsch (San Francisco: W. H. Freeman, 1981). I leave it to those two neurophysicians from Stonybrook to give the background, cite the studies, and record the exciting testimony, both pro and con, regarding the theory that each half of the brain makes a unique and special contribution to the way we think. Two of the best books on the practical application of the research are both by Tony Buzan, *Use Both Sides of Your Brain* (New York: E. P. Dutton, 1976) and *Make the Most of Your Mind* (New York: Linden Press/ Simon & Schuster, 1984.)
2. Sagan, *Dragons of Eden,* p. 161.
3. This comparison of daylight stars to our Western ignorance of the right hemisphere is from Prof. Robert Ornstein of the Langley Porter Neuropsychiatric Institute in San Francisco. Prof. Ornstein has done an enormous amount of research on the thinking specialties of the hemispheres; it was he who first measured, through EEG's, the brain waves of students who were doing figures, composing letters, daydreaming, and so forth. Many of the ideas in this chapter are based on Ornstein's findings.
4. Betty Edwards, *Drawing on the Right Side of the Brain* (Los Angeles: J. P. Tarcher, 1979), 55.

CHAPTER 5: BRANCHING: THE WHOLE-BRAINED WAY TO ORGANIZE YOUR MATERIAL

1. I refer you to Buzan, *Use Both Sides of Your Brain*, especially the chapter "Brain Patterns—Advanced Methods and Uses," pages 97 to 107.

CHAPTER 7: ASSERTIVENESS TRAINING: DEALING WITH THE CALIBAN CRITIC

1. Julian Jaynes, *The Origin of Consciousness in the Breakdown of the Bicameral Mind* (Boston: Houghton Mifflin, 1976), 98.
2. Willis Harman, Ph.D., and Howard Rheingold, *Higher Creativity: Liberating the Unconsciousness for Breakthrough Insights* (Los Angeles: J. P. Tarcher, 1984), 98.

CHAPTER 8: RE-VISION: CALIBAN RETURNS, AT YOUR INVITATION

1. Quoted in the *Writer's Digest Diary* (Cincinnati: Writer's Digest Books, 1981), 12.
2. Quoted in innumerable sources, including *Time*, May 12, 1986, 39.
3. The example is from *Plain English for Lawyers*, by Richard C. Wydick (Durham, N.C.: Carolina Academic Press, 1979), 10. Wydick is himself an attorney, so he is sensitive to the exactness of language required by the law, as well as the debt to clarity. Every lawyer should have a copy of this excellent book within easy grab.
4. William Strunk, Jr., and E. B. White, *Elements of Style*, 3rd ed. (New York: Macmillan, 1979), 73.
5. Fog Index is a service mark of Gunning-Mueller Clear Writing Institute, Inc., Santa Barbara, California. The Fog Index instructions have been adapted from "How to Take the Fog Out of Writing," by Robert Gunning and Douglas Mueller, © 1985 by Gunning-Mueller Clear Writing Institute, Inc., Santa Barbara, CA 93110.
6. *Apple II Reference Manual* (Cupertino, Calif.: Apple Computer, 1979), 92. Written by Christopher Espinosa.
7. See *Influencing with Integrity: Management Skills for Communication and Negotiation*, by Genie Z. Laborde (Palo Alto, Calif.: Syntony, 1984). Matching verbs and other language is only one part of the NLP communication model.
8. *San Diego Performing Arts Magazine*, October 1984.
9. Lee Iacocca, with William Novak, *Iacocca: An Autobiography* (New York: Bantam, 1984), 229.

CHAPTER 9: GOING TO THE MOVIES: CREATIVE VISUALIZATION AND WRITING

1. John Leo, "How the Hostages Came Through," *Time*, February 9, 1981, 52.
2. It sounds more like something Yogi Berra might say, but, according to *Time*, August 15, 1983, the remark belongs to Wohlford.
3. Sondra Perl and Arthur Egendorf, "The Process of Creative Discovery: Theory, Research, and Implications for Teaching," in Donald McQuade, ed., *Linguistics, Stylistics, and the Teaching of Composition*, Studies in Contemporary Language, No. 2, University of Akron, Department of English, 1979, 118–34. The underlying thesis of their research is that you have the answer inside your own head without knowing (yet) how to articulate it. Perl and Egendorf point out that "many thinkers since Kant have claimed that all valid thought and expression are rooted in the wider realm of pre-representational experience." Yet, "for all their concern with the realm beyond, even such powerful thinkers as Wittgenstein and Heidegger have not made clear *how* we have this realm available to us."
4. Eugene T. Gendlin and Linda Olsen, "The Use of Imagery in Experiential Focusing," *Psychotherapy: Theory, Research and Practice* (Winter 1970): 221–23.
5. Chuck Loch, "How to Feed Your Brain and Develop Your Creativity," *Writer's Digest*, vol. 61, no. 2, (February 1981), 20–25.
6. François Rochaix, the stage director of the Seattle Opera's production of *Die Walküre*, quoted one week before opening night in the *Weekly*, July 17–23, 1985, 35.
7. These were some of the responses from a group of third-graders: "I was with Haydn again today. He told me I must practice more to get better. He said that I must look

at the notes and then I would get a new book." "As I breathed in I felt like I was going down the steps. Then I found myself going into the sea and Neptune taught me how to swim." "I wanted to practice running and my teacher was Bruce Jenner. He said, 'Keep your pace and keep running.'" Reprinted with permission from Maureen Murdoch, M.A., M.F.C.C.; *Spinning Inward*, p. 79; 121 Wavecrest Avenue, Venice, CA 90291.

8. Loch, "How to Feed Your Brain," 25.

APPENDIX 1: SPELLING THROUGH VISUALIZATION

1. Edward Bernard Fry, Jacqueline K. Polk, and Dona Fountoukidis, *The Reading Teacher's Book of Lists* (Englewood Cliffs, N.J.: Prentice-Hall, 1984).
2. Fry, et. al., *Lists*, p. 57.
3. See Linda Verlee Williams, *Teaching for the Two-Sided Mind* (Englewood Cliffs, N.J.: Prentice-Hall, 1983), and Barbara Meister Vitale, *Unicorns Are Real: A Right-Brained Approach to Learning* (Rolling Hills: Jalmar Press, 1984), for more information.

APPENDIX 2: WRITING ON BOTH SIDES OF THE BRAIN WITH A WORD PROCESSOR

1. Donald Murray, "Writing and Teaching for Surprise," *College English* 46 (January 1984), 1.
2. For example, see such "outline processors" as KAMAS, Thoughtline, and Idea! and the prose check, Rightwriter, which analyzes text for errors in grammar, usage, punctuation, style, and spelling. Rightwriter marks clichés, slang, jargon, and the passive voice, and it also calculates a readability index similar to the Fog Index.